MW00652580

24 PATTERNS OF WISDOM

Other books by Anthony Lawlor

The Temple in the House
A Home for the Soul
Two As One (with Sherrie Lovler)

Ink Monkey Press
PO Box 11435
Santa Rosa, CA 95406
www.inkmonkey.com

Copyright © 2011 by Anthony Lawlor
Illustrations copyright © 2011 by Anthony Lawlor

All rights reserved. No part of this book may be reproduced or transmitted in any form or by any means, electronic or mechanical, including photocopying, recording, or by any information storage and retrieval system, without permission from the Publisher.

Title font: Brioso

ISBN 978-0-9840172-0-1

First Printing

Printed in China

1 3 5 7 9 10 8 6 4 2

24 PATTERNS OF WISDOM

Navigating the challenges and awakenings of
the human journey

Written and illustrated by
Anthony Lawlor

Ink Monkey Press

For Sherrie Lovler

*With gratitude to the teachers and friends
supporting and guiding the way*

CONTENTS

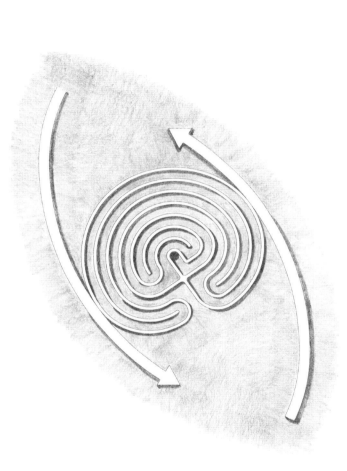

INTRODUCTION

*"You cannot solve a problem from the same consciousness
that created it. You must learn to see the world anew."*
— Albert Einstein

This book provides openings to "seeing the world anew." It presents 24 patterns of wisdom that map the road to finding out who you are, why you are here and where you are going. These patterns are visual diagrams of consciousness, illustrations that offer insight about where you are on your human journey and how one stage of experience grows into the others. This sequence of drawings helps free you from any single phase of development. It opens the way to engaging natural tides of change with greater happiness, peace and creativity.

The patterns of wisdom presented here provide essential understanding for navigating the world. To find our way takes all sorts of knowledge. We need varied and specific skills to make money, engage in a relationship, parent a child, cook a meal, write a poem and do the thousand other things that make a life. Through every pursuit, patterns of wisdom help us see what is happening and help us comprehend our connections to our surroundings. In contrast, lack of knowledge contracts us in fear and overwhelms us with confusion. When that happens, all the information in the universe cannot make things better. When we understand patterns of wisdom we feel expanded, peaceful and clear. We are more energized, imaginative and loving.

People throughout time have enhanced their knowledge by sensing the patterns that influence their thoughts and actions. When we understand this wisdom about the workings of life, we are better prepared to deal with each situation that arises. We can see what to avoid, what to embrace and when to remain neutral. Reference points can be found for steering a course through upheavals and down times. If we do not understand the patterns of wisdom shaping ourselves and the world, we become victims of circumstance. We can miss what is happening right in front of us and overlook clues about what is coming our way. Our actions can become mechanical, have limited effect and restrict our satisfaction.

24 Patterns of Wisdom provides tools for finding harmony in conflict, clarity in confusion, and comfort in chaos. By understanding the map of how wisdom transforms our lives, we discover what transforms the world. In random events, we can discern coherent sequences of development. Bombarded by swiftly changing information, we can find stability. In the radical reshuffling of society occurring in this century, we can be better prepared to maintain our true natures and stay connected to our authentic purposes.

The patterns of wisdom presented here are not rules for action or ideals for living. Instead, these visual diagrams of knowledge depict the unseen currents shaping who we are, what we do and where we go. Learning how to detect these patterns of wisdom alerts us to unconscious habits that can undermine us and put us in conflict with life. Having greater awareness of our autopilot actions allows us to be less dominated by worn out and rigid ways of thinking. It offers us greater freedom to choose how we want to live. Recognizing the wisdom in these diagrams improves our ability to see through surface appearances to the core of what shapes our lives. It opens the way to perceiving the wellsprings of inspiration at the heart of each situation.

The diagrams of wisdom on the following pages distill knowledge for living that has been developed through centuries of experience. Symbols and stories providing insights about the human journey are at the heart of every spiritual path, scientific discovery, psychological realization and artistic creation. Sacred teachings portray these revelations through the lives of Buddha, Christ and other sages. They depict them with images of the Wheel of Dharma, the Cross, the Star of David and other revered icons. Science describes this knowledge through formulas for gravity, the speed of light and the other forces structuring the universe. Psychologists convey this wisdom through archetypes of personal growth. Artists express this understanding through forms and colors that ignite vitality and inspire awe.

24 Patterns of Wisdom conveys this timeless knowledge in a unique way. It traces the path of growing wisdom through a new sequence of symbols. Each symbol depicts a stage in the process of gaining knowledge without referring to a particular religion or philosophy. Instead, this series of images depicts how our daily experience travels from the limits of the physical world to the freedom of consciousness shimmering through every detail of living.

The symbols illustrated here are archetypes of human experience. Archetypes are like the bones that give our bodies structure. They are essential, but unseen. Archetypes are the organizing principles that support and guide our emotions, actions and achievements. They are patterns that we fill with real-life experiences. Archetypes of life stages such as birth and death, are filled with the real-life experiences of our specific births and deaths. The archetypal roles of the Child, the Mother and the Hero are filled in with the details of our personal childhoods, our specific mothers and the particular heroic acts we encounter on our way. The archetypes of wisdom presented in this book describe essential patterns of experience such as the Circle of the Senses, the Primal Wound, the Belief Grid and Flowering.

Archetypes hover below the surface of every thought, word and action. We do not acquire them the way we acquire the knowledge of driving a car. Like the knowledge of breathing, the wisdom of archetypes is already guiding our lives. Yet, we can be unaware of the archetypes motivating and shaping us. To benefit from their guidance, we must learn to see and feel them. When we can directly experience these archetypes of wisdom and live in harmony with them, we can access the fullness and vitality of life.

Archetypes are not passive structures. They are vital links to the subtle, luminous forces that power our thoughts and gestures. These links are found at the overlaps between matter and energy, the interfaces where energy sparks matter alive. In this sense, archetypes are forms of potential, the readiness for action and achievement. Because archetypes already exist and are always behind everything we do, they are indestructible. Connection with them opens our lives to experience what is beyond change.

By learning to perceive archetypes, we learn the pathways

through which consciousness is expressed in us and our surroundings. Carl Jung, who developed the concept of psychological archetypes, said that whether we understand them or not, we must remain conscious of their influence. Archetypes are vital parts of nature and, therefore, connect us to our roots in the world. If we are cut off from these primordial images of existence, we are cut off from the profound richness of life.

By exploring archetypal wisdom, we not only enhance our personal journeys, we also connect to the rest of humanity. Joseph Campbell beautifully describes this experience in relation to the archetype of the Labyrinth: "Furthermore, we have not even to risk the adventure alone; for the heroes of all time have gone before us; the labyrinth is thoroughly known; we have only to follow the thread of the hero path. And where we had thought to find an abomination, we shall find a god; where we had thought to slay another, we shall slay ourselves; where we had thought to travel outward, we shall come to the center of our own existence; where we had thought to be alone, we shall be with all the world."

24 Patterns of Wisdom provides visual symbols you can use each day to guide and support your unique passage through the world. As you navigate the winding trail of day-to-day challenges, you can bring these images to mind as you would recall inspiring sayings and quotations to strengthen you with uplifting insights and motivating knowledge. By doing so, these 24 symbols become allies for making every step of your way a homecoming to the harmony, joy and abundance of your luminous nature.

1
OPENING

Within the joys and sorrows of living, openings to deeper vitality and inspiration can be found. Yet, the uncertainties of money and health, love and loss, obscure this richer experience of life. What we want can seem just beyond our reach. We may think that more wealth and more talent, better looks and better luck, are keys to greater happiness. The daily news, however, is filled with stories about people who appear to have everything and are still unhappy.

It is not the things we own that eclipse love, creativity and abundance. It is our inability to see through things and feel the energy and wisdom sparking them to life. As Joseph Campbell points out:

> *"People say that what we're all seeking is a meaning for life. I don't think that's what we're really seeking. I think what we're seeking is an experience of being alive, so that our life experiences on the purely physical plane will have resonance within our own innermost being and reality, so that we actually feel the rapture of being alive."*

The aliveness we seek, therefore, is reached by opening through physical forms to the vitality animating those forms. Touching this vitality, we feel the greater joy of living that Campbell describes.

We can feel the liveliness animating the physical world by opening to the consciousness moving and shaping it. Consciousness in this

Pattern of Wisdom 1 • Opening

Physical forms frame portals to the vitality and inspiration of consciousness.

context is the unseen organizing power giving form and usefulness to people and places. We experience consciousness as both active and silent. In its active currents, consciousness is an invisible combination of raw energy and the intelligence that guides the flow of that energy—just as the wind is unseen until it ripples a flag or sways the branches of a tree. Active consciousness animates the smiles and frowns, laughter and tears of the people we meet. It shapes and guides our reaction to those encounters.

Silent consciousness, on the other hand, is like the empty hub of a wheel. The hub provides an empty space that allows the spokes of the wheel to turn. In a similar way, we grasp the sides of a cup, but the hollow space within the cup makes it useful. We can sense thoughts, words and actions, we can touch people and places, but it is the space of silent consciousness that allows us to appreciate these experiences. If we do not acknowledge the relationship between silent consciousness and the physical forms of life, we get lost in those physical forms. Losing ourselves, we lose our freedom and happiness. On the other hand, experiencing silent consciousness within and around people and places sparks the joy of being alive. Because silent consciousness is spacious and unmoving, it is free from the births and deaths, gains and losses that can obscure our vitality and joy.

The drawing of Pattern of Wisdom 1, Opening illustrates how a pattern of perception frames the vitality of consciousness. The lighter ring in the drawing depicts a basic pattern underlying an object such as a window or a person's eye. The window and the eye are physical forms with practical functions. They frame the light that brings them to life. In this way, the physical forms of people and places frame the consciousness animating them. This consciousness is depicted by the gray background within and around the lighter circle.

To understand how this pattern works, we can see what Sarah learned from studying sculpture. At first, she focused on the visible forms of faces and objects. She did not notice the consciousness

Pattern of Wisdom 1, Opening diagrams how a physical form frames consciousness.

animating physical shapes. By not connecting to the invisible power behind the visible forms, her sculptures were lifeless. They lacked the artistry to infuse clay with life. No matter how expertly she crafted wood and stone, her work was devoid of inspiration.

One day, Sarah read a quote from her favorite sculptor, Andy Goldsworthy, that changed everything:

"I want to get under the surface. When I work with a leaf, rock, stick, it is not just that material in itself, it is an opening into the processes of life within and around it. When I leave it, these processes continue."

In an instant, Sarah realized what she had been missing. She looked beyond the visible surface of people and objects and saw the invisible consciousness animating them. Eyes and lips, fingers and forearms became more than interesting shapes. They sparked to life because they expressed energy and intelligence. Even mundane forms, like socks and spoons, glowed when she acknowledged how they revealed the forces within them.

Because consciousness is invisible, Sarah realized that visible forms are the only way to indicate its presence. It was like ocean waves indicating the direction and speed of the energy moving through them. What she ate and where she lived revealed the currents of life rippling through her world. To create the sculpture she dreamed of, she had to learn to see consciousness arising in buildings and bridges, boulders and trees, clothing and cars.

Sarah also wanted to see how physical objects pointed beyond themselves to the consciousness enlivening them. As she explored the links between consciousness and visible form, she discovered that her sculptures became more inspiring when they framed silent spaces. The effect was like a stone archway framing a blue sky. The physical limits of her art opened to the limitless consciousness shimmering through it.

What animated Sarah's sculpture also inspired her daily life. She began to experience her thoughts, words and actions framing silent consciousness. Whether her moods were happy or sad, peaceful or agitated, they flowed through a silent space of consciousness. This silent awareness watched the flow of life, but was unchanged by it. Noticing silent consciousness in and around herself opened the limits of her life to what was beyond limits. Everything she experienced arose from the space of silent consciousness. Recognizing this, her loneliness opened to connection. Her frustration became a creative conversation with the world. Through the changes that life brought each day, Sarah remained connected to the silent consciousness that did not change. As she opened to more peace, connection and creativity, she became more vital and alive. As she sensed consciousness in all things, her days became explorations of the luminous wisdom sculpting her and her surroundings.

• **Sense openings to consciousness in form.**
Pattern of Wisdom 1, Opening illustrates how a physical form frames an opening to consciousness. To experience this, compare the circle in the drawing to the circular iris of a friend's eye. Perceive the circle of the pattern of Opening hovering just behind the physical circle of the iris. Sense the circle of the iris framing the spark of life, the consciousness, animating your friend's eye. Experience the pattern of Opening within other framing forms such as windows, doorways or a break in the clouds. In these openings, feel the aliveness of silent consciousness.

2

SELF AWARENESS

Pattern of Wisdom 2, Self Awareness illustrates consciousness revolving within itself and generating a seed of potential. When our attention turns to notice itself, a kernel of possibilities emerges. These kernels of energy sprout into the thoughts and actions that shape our world. We experience this as ideas rising in our minds. We notice an idea and take action to convert that impulse of consciousness into physical form. For example, an idea for breakfast might arise. We notice this idea, go to the kitchen, mix cereal and milk in a bowl and enjoy our breakfast. Simply noticing that we exist turns the broad potential of consciousness into seeds of desire and the plans that can fulfill them.

Recognizing consciousness within us is similar to the process of sap cycling through an apple tree and producing apple seeds. As consciousness cycles through our minds, it generates seed after seed of thought. Each thought is a kernel of awareness filled with energy and wisdom. These thought seeds of energy and knowledge cycle into the constant stream of words, actions and relationships that form our lives. We experience these kernels of consciousness in the *I AM* behind our perceptions and the *I DO* behind our actions.

The architect Frank Lloyd Wright used a creative process that embodied this pattern of wisdom. He understood the importance of perceiving consciousness reflecting upon itself to generate a seed idea that contained all the qualities of a home. He often gave the houses

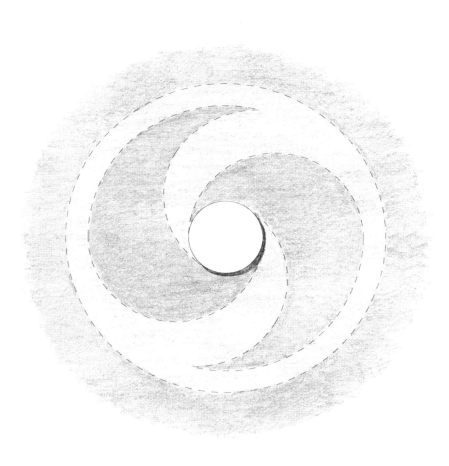

Pattern of Wisdom 2 • Self Awareness

Turning within to recognize consciousness spawns seeds of potential.

he designed names such as Wingspread and Hollyhock House. The name of the home reflected the kernel of the architect's consciousness. From this kernel grew all the choices for the floor plan, building materials, colors and other elements. One of Wright's houses, called Fallingwater, was built over a waterfall. Everything about the design, from its cascading terraces to its rough stone walls, echoed the flowing stream and the limestone bluff where the house was built.

Another example of this pattern of wisdom comes from Paul, a chef, who earned acclaim for creating meals attuned to the cycles of nature. Each morning, he found seeds of inspiration for his menus by walking to his restaurant through Central Park. Rain or shine, summer or winter, he took plenty of time to stroll down the paths. Every day he followed a different route and let his intuition guide him. As he wandered under a row of arching trees or along the edge of a pond, Paul moved toward whatever called to him. He might be attracted to the curve of a footbridge, the spray of a fountain or a cluster of red autumn leaves. His attention might be drawn to the song of a Cape May Warbler or a street singer playing the blues, the aroma of roasting peanuts or blooming honeysuckle. Within each setting, he watched the passing faces, sensed their moods and noted the styles of their clothing. He opened his mind to these sights, sounds and aromas, and let them flood his senses. When Paul was filled with inspiration, he sat on a bench and recalled the experiences he had gathered. Within this silent moment, he noticed the images rising in his awareness. They might include the six-pointed star of a crocus, a golden shaft of morning light or rain glistening on a stone. He looked for a thread connecting these images. It could be a geometric shape, a color or an aroma. Weaving his mind through these experiences, a theme would appear. Some examples were Autumn Smoke, Winter Crunch, Summer Night, Moon Song and Equinox Dance. Each theme provided the seed of consciousness indicating the ingredients for that night's menu. With this reference seed in mind, Paul selected the vegetables, grains, meats, cheeses, spices, wines and other elements that embodied the theme. This kernel of consciousness guided the ways he combined the ingredients to create innovative and sumptuous meals.

In daily life, seeds of Self Awareness contain the character traits we express. They hold the ways we speak and act, the foods and places we prefer. They contain our responses to art and the news. These seeds of potential influence whether we enact loving or combative relationships. They indicate if we become lone visionaries or team players. Noticing the seeds of our characters reveals the wisdom of what is true for us amidst the thousands of choices life presents.

• *Observe seeds of potential arising within you.*
Pattern of Wisdom 2, Self Awareness depicts consciousness turning within itself and spawning a seed of potential. Use this pattern whenever you want to generate new ideas. Sit quietly and notice the thoughts circling within your mind. Allow the challenge you are facing to flow into your attention. Let the challenge turn within your mind until a seed of inspiration emerges. Explore the seed and discover the wisdom it contains.

3

CIRCLE OF THE SENSES

Pattern of Wisdom 3, Circle of the Senses illustrates how we project our attention toward a scene such as a mountain creek and feel the potential of consciousness through our senses. In the process, we discover how consciousness moves through us to discern the flowing water, the granite boulders and the overhanging plants that describe the creek. Listening to the creek's gurgling rhythms, we find consciousness extending through our ears to savor the nuances of sound. Directing our senses toward the fragrance of the forest, the rough bark of the trees and the sweetness of a trail snack, we learn how consciousness notices the inflections of aroma, texture and taste. Each ray of perception reveals less about the things we experience and more about the capacity of consciousness to sense them through our bodies and minds.

Scientifically, information from the surroundings enters our senses and is processed by our brains. Yet, in any situation countless sights and sounds present themselves. Within this abundance of impulses, we direct our attention to what is personally important to us. Out of all the food in the market, we choose what satisfies our individual tastes. William Blake observed that life "leads you to believe a lie when you see with, not through, the eye." Usually, our minds are dominated by the people, objects and places we focus upon. We pay attention to a friend's complaints, a snow-covered sidewalk and the

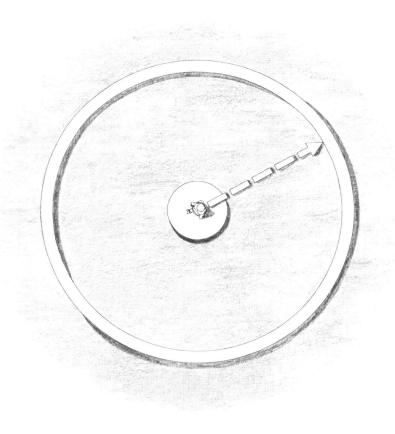

Pattern of Wisdom 3 • Circle of the Senses

Within the ring of perception, we discover the traits of consciousness.

lentil soup we ate for lunch. These combinations of sound and form are experienced in the rays of consciousness flowing through us into the surroundings. If we slept all day, the recognition of this flowing consciousness would be dimmed and these sensations would cease to exist. On the other hand, noticing a ray of attention radiating through our eyes toward a flower enlivens the process of perception. As we sense consciousness reaching out to meet the flower, its colors become more vivid and we feel more alive.

As the rays of our senses project into the surroundings, they encounter limits. Walking through a forest, we see as far as the trees encircling us. Sailing an ocean, our rays of sight extend to the horizon and stars. In a restaurant, our perception reaches to the sights and sounds filling the room. The limits of sensory experience mark the Circle of the Senses.

At the center of the Circle of the Senses, we inhabit the viewpoint of the Seer—the person sensing the surroundings. At the edge of the

*As the Seer, we occupy
the center of our perception.*

circle, we sense Seen objects—the people and places we encounter. The Seer and the Seen are linked through the Process of Seeing—the consciousness passing through us to experience the world. Usually, Seen objects obscure the Process of Seeing.

When Isaac, a photographer, stood in Times Square on New Year's Eve, the towering buildings, flashing signs, crushing crowds and honking horns dominated his awareness. His Process of Seeing was obscured by the cacophony of sights and sounds. The following spring, Isaac walked through Central Park. The flowering trees, fragrant breezes and trotting joggers overshadowed his perception with sensations of delight.

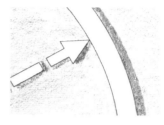

Seen objects define the outer rim of the Circle of the Senses.

When physical objects overwhelmed Isaac's perception, as they did in Times Square, his energy and joy were obscured. Material circumstances determined his happiness or sadness. A rainy day put him in a rainy mood. A sunny afternoon brightened his day. If the stock market soared then plunged, his emotions climbed and tumbled with it. His life lurched back and forth from one drama to another.

On the other hand, when Isaac experienced himself as the Seer within the Circle of the Senses, he was less influenced by what he saw. Instead of being the victim of events, he became creatively engaged with the consciousness flowing through him. Rather than feeling trapped in a traffic jam, he sat in the stream of cars sensing the play of light and shadow, the rhythms of radio tunes and the quiet moments of alone time. Standing in the market checkout line changed from a frustrating delay into an exploration of consciousness sensing the passing faces, the bins of brightly colored vegetables and the well-stocked shelves. Cheering his daughter's soccer team went from being an emotional roller coaster to an exciting discovery of consciousness radiating through him to sense the play of competing forces.

When Isaac stood in a room, a public plaza or a wilderness canyon, he noticed how the surrounding walls limited the distance he could see. As the Seer, he occupied the center of his Circle of the Senses. The consciousness radiating through his eyes to enact the Process of Seeing linked him to the outer limits of his circle. Wherever Isaac went, his experiences took place within the

In the Process of Perception, we sense the flow of consciousness through us to experience the world.

Circle of the Senses. Every perception involved this combination of Seer, Seen and Processing of Seeing.

Over time, Isaac noticed the Seer functioning on two levels, active and silent. As an active Seer, he experienced the world with his senses and emotions. There was also a silent level within him that quietly observed what happened. The active level of experience could be described. But nothing could describe the silent consciousness within the Seer. He noticed that this silent consciousness was always present, quietly observing the scene. It did not change in response to changes in seeing, hearing, touching or smelling. He compared this silent consciousness of the Seer to an alert space within which his thoughts and his emotions flowed. It was like the space in a room that people walked through. No matter what activities passed through the room, the space did not change.

As the silent Seer became more prominent in the circle of Isaac's senses, he found more stability within change. Friends might visit and leave. News of the world streamed through the media. Colors, sounds, textures, aromas and flavors flowed through his senses. Ideas and emotions arose and disappeared in his mind. All of it swirled through the quiet, unmoving space of the silent Seer.

The more Isaac noticed the consciousness of the silent Seer, the more vivid his experiences of life became. By opening to unchanging consciousness, he sensed richer dimensions of changing sights and sounds. When he fully relaxed into the silent level of the Seer, he understood what William Blake meant when he said, "If the doors of perception were cleansed, everything would appear as it is, infinite."

• *Feel consciousness in your Circle of the Senses.* Pattern of Wisdom 3, Circle of the Senses depicts how we can experience consciousness through the process of perception. Use this pattern to imagine yourself as the Seer standing at the center of your Circle of the Senses. Perceive the Seen objects around you as the outer ring of the circle. Sense the rays of your perception extending through you to a seen object such as a tree. Experience the branches and rustling leaves as the traits of consciousness seeing and hearing the tree. Notice if your perception becomes more vivid. In the middle of a hectic moment, remember to stop and reframe the scene. Become the Seer at the center of your Circle of the Senses. From that calm, unmoving stance observe what is happening. Feel the stability in the middle of change.

4
SELF and OTHER

Pattern of Wisdom 4, Self and Other depicts consciousness appearing to divide into two circles of identity through the process of perception. At the center of one circle, we assume the role of the "Self." At the center of the second circle, we label individuals the "Other." The circles of Self and Other overlap and influence one another. You have one circle of family, friends and interests while your neighbor has another circle of life. Where the two circles interact determines your relationship with your neighbor. If she cooks a delicious stew for dinner that spreads enticing aromas into your apartment, your Circle of Self is enriched. If your neighbor blasts heavy metal music at two o'clock in the morning, your Circle of Self is probably irritated.

Elena noticed the pattern of Self and Other shaping her experiences. Walking down Market Street, her mood changed each time her Circle of Self encountered the circle of another person. When her circle overlapped the circle of a homeless woman, Elena felt a combination of compassion and contraction. Her heart went out to the woman, but her body tensed. Crossing paths with a street musician, Elena felt both delight and melancholy. When she met her boyfriend, Brian, she glowed with the memory of a wonderful weekend they had spent by the sea. Yet, sadness clouded her circle when she recalled a disagreement they had earlier that week.

When the circle of Elena's senses overlapped another person's,

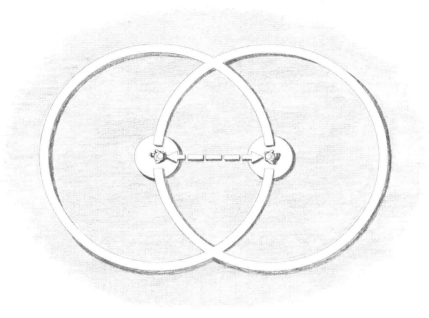

Pattern of Wisdom 4 • Self and Other

The process of perception appears to divide consciousness into opposites.

she saw capacities of consciousness being revealed. Hope and fear, inspiration and disappointment came forward. When she jogged through the park, her interactions with nature revealed the wonder, connection and beauty that she did not experience when she was isolated from the earth.

As Elena's Circle of Self met the Circle of Other in Brian, she saw reflections of her consciousness. By engaging his humor and insecurity, she learned about her humor and insecurity. His tenderness toward her opened her tenderness to herself and reflected it back to him.

On a trip to Rome, Elena saw how interactions between Self and Other brought out varied viewpoints of consciousness and discovered different facets of a place. Following her passion for design, she walked through the city studying the ancient buildings. Brian, on the other hand, loved cooking and focused on the abundant variety of foods and spices he found in different neighborhoods. At the end of each day, Elena and Brian sat in a cafe and shared what they had experienced. Together, they discovered the textures of consciousness expressing itself as the architecture and food of the city. Sharing the world from two viewpoints enriched their Circles of Self and Other.

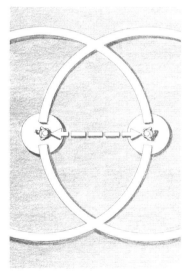

The pattern Self and Other reveals diverse traits of consciousness.

At other times, the interaction of their circles appeared to split consciousness into conflict. Elena's hopes for love with Brian were tinged with fears of rejection. His conservative political beliefs contradicted her progressive views and his strict scientific attitude dismissed her spiritual experiences. Sometimes it seemed that his Circle of Other constantly tested the interests of her Circle of Self.

Paradoxically, in the pattern of Self and Other, Elena sensed consciousness being at once unified and divided. The mingling of the two circles enlivened and detracted from both. Through this pattern of wisdom, she experienced two apparently opposite identities arising from one shimmering consciousness.

• *Feel Self and Other shaping your experience.*

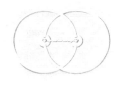

Pattern of Wisdom 4, Self and Other illustrates perception appearing to split consciousness into two identities. To experience this, imagine yourself standing at the center of your Circle of Self and a friend at the center of her Circle of Other. Sense the feeling in your circle shifting when it overlaps with your friend's circle. Feel your experience changing when your circle mingles with a different person's. In a conversation, sense how divergent viewpoints reveal varied qualities of consciousness such as happiness and sadness. Sense Self and Other as two aspects of one consciousness coming alive.

5

PRIMAL WOUND

Pattern of Wisdom 5, Primal Wound illustrates how a gap appears to open in consciousness by dividing the Circle of Self from the Circle of Other. Perceiving this split, our Circle of Self can feel diminished. The Circle of Other seems to violate our territory. Our sense of wholeness shakes. Since every interaction with life is an encounter with the Circle of Other, the painful gap between the two circles can seem to permeate every experience. We feel this gap as the Primal Wound.

Eli experienced the pattern of the Primal Wound as an empty void. He sensed a piece of his life getting lost in the gap between himself and others. The fear of being consumed by this painful division hovered in the background of everything he did. He attempted to avoid this emotional ache by distracting himself through any means possible. One way he did this was by creating drama. Interacting with friends and coworkers, he contradicted whatever they said. He was more interested in arguing and winning than discussing and exploring. He found countless ways to criticize others and ignite fights. Worry was another way he tried to evade the pain of the Primal Wound. His mind whirled with anxiety about money, health, his kids, climate change and world politics. Entertainment offered another escape. He buried himself in books, movies, video games and golf. At meals, he numbed himself with too much food and alcohol.

The distractions did not work. Eli was troubled by a nagging

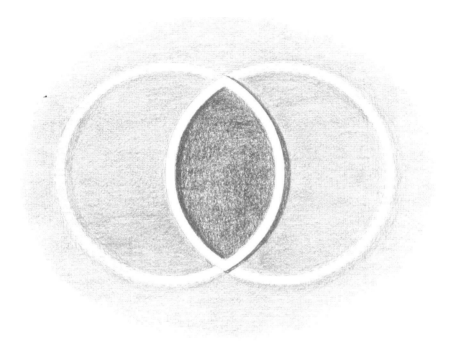

Pattern of Wisdom 5 • Primal Wound

Splitting Self from Other appears to open a painful gap in consciousness.

sense of isolation and disconnection from his family, friends and society. An emotional homelessness clouded his every move. Through the lens of the Primal Wound, Eli's world became a fragmented collection of competing parts. His interests struggled with those of his neighbors. His country fought against others. He saw humans battling nature.

As a result, the pain of the Primal Wound continued to ache through every interaction. Even the most fulfilling achievements in business carried with them a

The Primal Wound turns the human journey into a quest for healing.

quality of being "wonderful, but...." His daughter's wedding was perfect except for his drunken uncle who made one obnoxious joke after another. His sister's art exhibit got rave reviews, but none of the paintings sold. Beset by this sense of lack, every encounter aggravated his experience of the Primal Wound.

Burdened by a painful sense of injury and unfulfilled longing, Eli's life turned into a quest for healing. He ate a healthier diet and worked out at the gym. To mend his emotions, he visited a therapist, meditated daily and spent three days in the desert on a vision quest. Working his way through healers and spiritual techniques, he searched for methods to restore his sense of totality. He hunted for more soulfulness in his relationships, more meaningful work, more harmony with his community and deeper communion with nature. As long as he saw a gap between himself and others, however, the pain of the Primal Wound throbbed within him.

Even though the ache did not disappear, Eli felt more alive when he experienced consciousness moving through the gap between himself and others. By sensing this divide as a pattern of energy and intelligence, the nagging pain did not feel locked into a static state. The life force breathed beneath the surface of current conditions, inspiring him across the difficult gap.

• *Feel the effects of the Primal Wound.*

 Pattern of Wisdom 5, Primal Wound illustrates how dividing Self from Other appears to open a painful gap in consciousness. Experience this pattern by imagining yourself at the center of your Circle of Self and a friend at the center her Circle. Notice the gap between you. Sense any pain or fear connected with this gap. Are there ways you attempt to avoid this pain or fear? If so, do they involve drama, worry, entertainment, overeating, fantasizing or other types of escape? Have you attempted to heal the ache of this divide? If so, how? Despite the pain of the Primal Wound, sense consciousness moving through the gap. Feel the energy and intelligence of consciousness enlivening the divided places in your life.

29

6
HEALING WOMB

Pattern of Wisdom 6, Healing Womb illustrates how entering the Primal Wound reconnects us with the harmony and vitality of an undivided field of consciousness. Dwelling within the Primal Wound, emptiness and conflict can seem to be everywhere. We long for the fullness of light, love and abundance. Once the Circle of Self is wounded, however, painful gaps appear all around us. Each encounter with a friend, no matter how interesting or encouraging, has some missed communication or subtle conflict. Every restaurant, store or park, no matter how exciting or beautiful, has some discomfort or irritation. Each movie, concert or baseball game, no matter how thrilling or inspiring, has moments of dead space and failure. Freedom encounters restrictions. Love is undermined by disagreements. Health is weakened by aging and illness. Creativity gets blocked. Escaping from this dilemma seems impossible. At times, we may lose hope of ever being free of the pain.

Eli felt trapped in the Primal Wound. He visited a counselor who encouraged him to face his emotional ache. The idea frightened him. How could entering a painful injury bring healing? The counselor pointed out that Eli already encountered the Primal Wound at every turn. Reluctantly, Eli admitted he could no longer deny or avoid his pain. With the counselor's guidance, he opened his heart and mind to his psychological wound. It was scary. He wanted to run. Every cell in

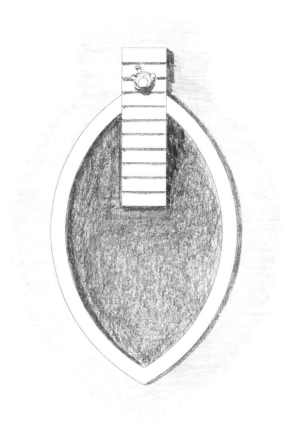

Pattern of Wisdom 6 • Healing Womb

Within the Primal Wound is an unbroken space of vitality and renewal.

31

his body resisted engaging the emptiness aching within him.

To Eli's surprise, entering the Primal Wound did not destroy him. The jaws of division that threatened to rip him in two did not close. In the gap between the dividing forces, he discovered a single space of unbroken consciousness. What appeared to be shattered and isolated shards of life were actually connected by an unseen spacious consciousness. The gap between Self and Other was not an injury. This opening framed a deeper, richer experience of oneness. What looked like battling parts were, in fact, two halves of one whole. The split between Eli and others was not a split after all. A single consciousness reflected itself through them to reveal a more vibrant unity. The wound that threatened a painful, shredded end became an opening to a new, more vibrant beginning.

Eli came to experience the pattern of the Primal Wound as a Healing Womb. What had appeared to be a chasm of pain and death became a dynamic space of rebirth and renewal. He learned to see the overlapping circles of Self and Other framing the silent totality of consciousness. The oppositions of this structure served to resonate consciousness toward flowing energy and wisdom. What was abstract potential became a wellspring of primal forces, a bubbling source of fresh forms of living.

Near his house, Eli found the pattern of the Healing Womb in the architecture of a church. Within the old stone sanctuary, he saw physical symbols of separation creating a unified space for easing his pain and restoring his spirit. The portal divided the active consciousness of daily life from the quieter consciousness of a protected place. It broke the facade of the building and allowed him to access the healing space. Like the mouth of a huge being, the portal devoured those entering the church, not to injure them, but to create a place of renewal. Inside the sanctuary, the walls separated the roof from the floor to define a womb space for healing. Between the light and shadow within this gap, Eli sensed a lively peace. Entering this open space, the ache of his Primal Wound became the pattern of a Healing Womb, a place that gave birth to a more dynamic totality of connection and delight.

• *Find Healing Wombs within Primal Wounds.* Pattern of Wisdom 6, Healing Womb depicts entering the Primal Wound to find an unbroken field of vitality and renewal. Experience this by sensing the gap separating you from a friend. In this gap, notice if you feel emptiness and longing. If so, sense the emotional ache associated with this gap. Imagine walking down a flight of steps into this emotional pain. Notice if resistance arises. Imagine descending through this resistance and entering the painful gap. Within this gap, sense the silent space. Feel the unbroken unity of consciousness within this silent space. Sense its dynamic peace and renewal.

7

BELIEF GRID

Pattern of Wisdom 7, Belief Grid illustrates our tendency to create a framework of concepts to help us navigate the world. We use this pattern when something breaks and we rush to explain it. As soon as a tornado or earthquake shatters a town, experts appear on the news. With diagrams and descriptions they give us the who, what, when, where and why of the crisis. After a personal loss such as a divorce or the death of a spouse, we also create stories to explain what happened. The tales we tell describe the characters and forces that threw our lives out of balance. They indicate how we hope to set things right and where they will go in the future. With frameworks of science, religion and other systems of thought, we put the people, places and events of life into understandable patterns. These mental maps help us navigate the terrain of living and avoid further injury.

When we recall the Primal Wound, we may think of the pain inflicted by splitting consciousness into Self and Other. To prevent experiencing that sting again, we search for a new structure that will support living in wholeness. To that end, we create a Belief Grid that will provide reliable reference points for living. With this framework of concepts, we hope to bring order to turmoil and guard against losing ourselves in a murky undertow of forces.

An architect named Becky used this pattern to develop a unique framework for creating houses. She began each design by drawing

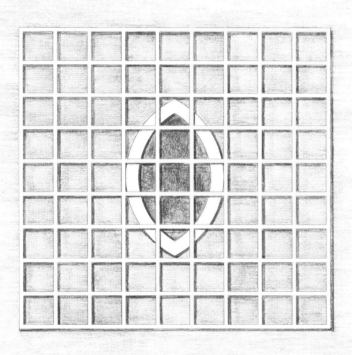

Pattern of Wisdom 7 • Belief Grid

Frameworks of belief shape and limit access to primal powers of renewal.

a 2-inch by 2-inch grid on a large sheet of paper. Then she would sit at her desk and gaze through the lines of this structure at the white space on the page. She brought to mind her client's needs and dreams. She thought about the building site, the climate and the budget for the project. Soon, images of the floor plan, the roof, the walls and the windows would appear within the gridwork of lines. Becky knew these architectural forms arose within her imagination, but the framework was her tool for teasing out the first stages of the design. With these rough images in mind, Becky used her grid to create the precise arrangement of the rooms in the floor plan. She believed her framework of lines enabled her to create harmonious and inspiring houses.

Since the grid helped her designwork, Becky unconsciously used a mental grid of beliefs and principles to improve her life. Her Belief Grid determined the value, quality and condition of everything she encountered. With it, she categorized the worth of each piece of clothing in her closet. The quality of a dress, for example, was judged to be excellent or inferior and whether it was to be worn for special occasions or everyday use. Through her Belief Grid, Becky graded books and movies as interesting or boring, creative or clichéd, significant or trivial. Her network of concepts gauged everything as beautiful or plain, fresh or worn out, valuable or a waste of time, logical or crazy.

Becky's Belief Grid measured the friendliness or antagonism of relatives, friends and coworkers. It determined the agreeable or irritating qualities of her community and the weather. The health of her food and effectiveness of her exercise were sifted through her framework of concepts. It located where she stood in the world and marked the position of her favorite restaurants, clothing stores, movie theaters and vacations spots.

Through her Belief Grid, Becky arranged the events of her life into predictable patterns. She categorized people by intelligence, sense of humor, reliability and thoughtfulness. Neighborhoods in her city were ranked from most to least livable. Her map of information described where she came from and where she was going. It made sense of her past and predicted her future. Within her mental chart of facts and figures, Becky found meaning and purpose, where she belonged and where she felt isolated, what made her happy and what caused sadness, what enhanced her wellbeing and what threw her into insecurity.

After Becky used the pattern of her Belief Grid to define what she could see, she used it to define what was invisible. Her framework of ideas gave whatever she could not name a recognizable label. Among this list were elusive experiences and concepts such as spirit, soul, God, the life force and transcendence.

The downside of Becky's Belief Grid was that it restrained her life. It limited the possible directions she allowed her architectural designs to take. Sometimes her controlling ideas caused her creativity to stagnate. Yet, her mind was a Belief Grid-making machine and she could not manage without its categories and measurements. Her framework of information helped her locate food, establish a home and choose clothing. It helped her to know the route from home to work, the price of apples and when a movie started. The problem came when she made the pattern of her Belief Grid more important than the energy and guidance of consciousness. Because Becky's Belief Grid only valued sleek modern architecture, she pressured clients that wanted traditional styles to change their tastes. If they resisted, she kept selling them her ideas until she got her way. Becky earned a reputation of being difficult to work with. As a result, she lost business. By making her Belief Grid more important than serving her clientele, she blocked the flow of income needed for her business to thrive. She came to resent her clients. Her emotions hardened and the pattern of her Belief Grid became a self-restricting cage.

Since Becky saw her Belief Grid as essential to her health and wellbeing, it clouded her interactions with others. Instead of relating human to human, her set of ideas interacted with the Belief Grid of each person she met. The possible interactions she could have were squeezed through her limited filter. It determined whether or not their beliefs agreed or conflicted with hers. In extreme cases, disagreements between Becky's Belief Grid and another person's ideas ignited arguments. The scaffold of concepts she used to improve her life could also make her miserable.

In another example of this pattern, a therapist named Nate used his knowledge of Belief Grids to work with couples who had relationship problems. To find out where a pair were out of sync, he had them write what they valued on two large grids which he placed side-by-side on his conference room wall. Within this framework, the couple described their concepts about money, sex, raising children, career, housework, healthcare, spirituality, places to live, music, art and sports. Looking at the two Belief Grids, Nate asked the couple to discuss which beliefs agreed and which beliefs conflicted. He asked them to talk about what values united them and what values pushed them apart. This framework of standards helped the couple explore where they supported one another and where they did not.

When the couple's patterns of beliefs were spread before them, Nate asked the pair to see their guiding values and principles as different forms of consciousness. He likened it to the different shapes of dishes, bowls and cups all made from one material, clay. The two were invited to look through the varied forms of their beliefs and feel the unity of consciousness connecting them. In this way, the couple experienced how they could honor both the differences and unity in their values. Their Belief Grids changed from being patterns that divided them to frameworks for connecting them.

• *Discover Belief Grids shaping your experience.* Pattern of Wisdom 7, Belief Grid depicts the frameworks of concepts we create to help us navigate the world. To discover your Belief Grid, draw a grid on a piece of paper. In the squares, write your beliefs about everything from love to global politics. Imagine viewing a person through your Belief Grid of values. Feel this framework of concepts shaping your opinion of this person. Experience the parts of your life where your system of values supports you and where it hinders you. Instead of seeing your Belief Grid as a network of rigid facts, experience it as consciousness taking on a pattern to discover its possibilities.

8

BLURRING

Pattern of Wisdom 8, Blurring depicts consciousness loosening the rigid boundaries of a Belief Grid. We may use a framework of concepts to box life into predictable patterns, but the primal powers of consciousness cannot be constrained for long. Beneath our clear definitions of the world pulsate vast and elusive currents. The measurements of our Belief Grids cannot compute the measureless powers flowing from the wellsprings of the Healing Womb. No single formula can calculate the span of the universe from grasshoppers to galaxies. No amount of detail can map the currents of the consciousness animating our lives. As Shakespeare observed, "There are more things in heaven and earth, Horatio, than are dreamt of in your philosophy."

The pattern of Blurring a Belief Grid occurred with the rise of Impressionism, the style of painting created by Claude Monet, Auguste Renior and other artists in France around 1860. Before Impressionism, painters of the Academy of the Beaux-Arts followed strict beliefs about what made a painting beautiful. The academics only painted historical and religious subjects and formal portraits. They did not depict landscapes. Their images were carefully finished and looked realistic when examined closely. All traces of brushstrokes were downplayed and the artist's personality, emotions and working techniques were concealed. The result was paintings that were unemotional and disconnected from daily concerns. Impressionist painters violated every

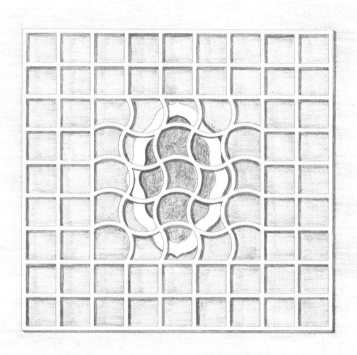

Pattern of Wisdom 8 • Blurring

The erosion of our Belief Grids connects us to revitalizing currents of consciousness.

one of the Academy's rules and values. The subjects of this style were common scenes of passing moments in daily life. Landscapes were often depicted. The images were roughly finished and did not look realistic when examined closely. Brushstrokes created prominent textures. The artist's emotions, personality and working techniques were expressed openly. When the Impressionists tried to exhibit their new style at the Academy's annual art show, their paintings clashed with the Belief Grid of established artistic taste. They were rejected as ugly and primitive. Even though the Impressionists blurred the framework of concepts that was popular at the time, their work soon prevailed. Their style was widely accepted and changed the way we experience art and life.

Despite the Blurring of our Belief Grids, we may persist in thinking that more information and greater effort will keep our definitions, and our lives, in neat rows. Melinda's college age daughter, Zoey, resisted her mother's plan that she study medicine. Instead, Zoey followed her passion for art. Melinda persisted in her scheme and bombarded her daughter with articles proving that being a doctor would keep Zoey financially stable and serve the greater good of society. Her daughter responded creatively by blurring the lines between art and science. She used medical x-rays of the brain as inspirations for a series of abstract paintings.

Before Zoey was born, Melinda based her happiness on her daughter becoming a doctor. The Blurring of this plan threatened to destroy Melinda's dream. Yet, the creative wellsprings inspiring Zoey's art were not agents of doom. They helped Melinda face her own lost dreams instead of pushing them on her daughter. Once she freed herself from this idea, Melinda studied herbal medicine and became a naturopath while Zoey heeded the call of her artistic soul.

Blurring the boundaries of Melinda's Belief Grid moved her limits into the flow of consciousness. In the same way that plucking guitar strings resonates silent air into melodies, the erosion of her framework of values pulsated consciousness into inspiring thoughts and actions. She no longer sensed the elusive forces eroding her Belief Grid as threats. They became the call of life to express itself though her. This call flowed in urges to break free of stifling concepts and fixed routines. Responding to these desires, she realized that fitting things into her Belief Grid did not make her feel more alive. Her framework of principles was an instrument that assisted her in exploring the mysteries of consciousness. Certainly, her mind cherished the practical functions of her Belief Grid, but relaxing her hold on rigid categories and measurements freed Melinda to experience more vital and creative ways of living.

• *Notice life Blurring your Belief Grid.*

Pattern of Wisdom 8, Blurring depicts consciousness loosening the rigid lines of a Belief Grid. See this pattern occurring in daily life by noticing how your best laid plans are often altered by unexpected events. Notice how Blurring your Belief Grid can guide you toward unforeseen benefits and open you to new, more expanded possibilities of experience.

9
FLUID WEB

Pattern of Wisdom 9, Fluid Web illustrates consciousness blurring a Belief Grid until the entire framework melts into a shimmering network of living. This process transforms a rigid framework of concepts, intended to restrict the ever-shifting currents of consciousness, into an undulating fabric of living that expresses them. The pattern of the Fluid Web receives the waves of energy rising and falling within the ocean of consciousness and guides them into vital forms and experiences. When a plunge in the stock market threatened Adam's portfolio, for example, it spurred a reorganization of his retirement plan. This reorganization allowed him to weather future turmoil. When ash clouds from an erupting volcano filled the skies over Iceland, Celeste and Jacob's flight was redirected from Germany to a beautiful part of Spain that they might never have visited. When Abby's noble ideal to love all beings was challenged by a driver who cut her off in traffic, she remembered the time she had done the same thing rushing her daughter to the hospital. The experience opened her to a new depth of compassion. If Caitlin hadn't been fired from a job she hated, she might not have started the organic bakery that expressed her talents. In the overturning of our well-crafted policies, intelligent strategies, helpful programs, balanced routines and time-tested methods, the Fluid Web shimmers with renewing energy and knowledge.

Marco experienced the pattern of the Fluid Web during his di-

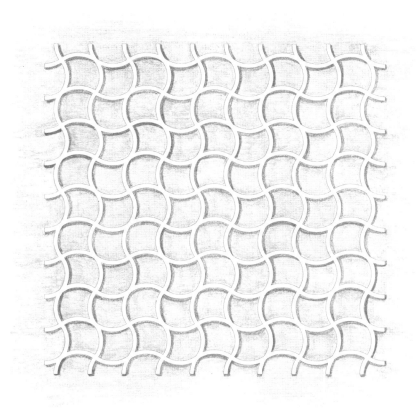

Pattern of Wisdom 9 • Fluid Web

Blurred frameworks of belief melt into flexible fields of vital possibility.

vorce. His Belief Grid had provided the solid foundation for predictable living. This conceptual framework did not, however, withstand the dissolution of his marriage. Losing love was painful. The destruction of his Belief Grid felt like death. The life he had planned dissolved, but he continued trying to plug everything into his Belief Grid. In the Fluid Web of his new circumstances, however, nothing remained fixed. When Marco started dating again, he carried old beliefs about the roles of men and women with him. No one fit his failed framework. Time after time, his old concepts prevented him from connecting with potential partners. By clinging to what was out of touch with his new life, he passed through one disappointing relationship after another. Only after giving up his former rigid beliefs and opening to more flexible ways of thinking did he discover a new love.

Within the Fluid Web, the logical rules of Marco's Belief Grid no longer applied. His clear ideas dividing true from false dissolved into shades of gray. Mental walls separating friends from enemies, fact from fiction, needs from wants, gains from losses, order from chaos, and creation from destruction crumbled into elusive, ever-shifting relationships. When his divorce plunged him into depression, a lifelong friend recoiled and abandoned him. When he was pressured to meet a major deadline at work, a fierce enemy in his office extended a helping hand and showed surprising understanding for what Marco was going through. When his former reliance on facts and statistics merged with a new found passion for poetry, it increased the power of the articles he wrote for a science journal.

Marco compared the melting of his Belief Grid to moving from living on land to sailing the ocean. His methods for living on solid ground did not apply to navigating the ever-shifting sea. On land, his house stayed in one place. On the sea, his sailboat moved with the tides. On land, he traveled in straight lines by generating his own power. On the sea, he traveled in zigzags by catching the power of the wind. On land, he navigated by the grid of streets. On the sea, he navigated by the sun and the field of stars. On land, relationships were fixed. On the sea, they shifted from moment to moment. On land, he found safety in stability. On the sea, safety came from responding to ever-changing circumstances. On land, he focused on having a fixed place for everything. On the sea, he focused on exploring new places and discovering new possibilities.

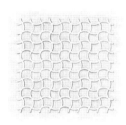

• ***Sense Belief Grids melting into Fluid Webs.*** Pattern of Wisdom 9, Fluid Web illustrates consciousness dissolving the rigid lines of your Belief Grid into an shimmering network of consciousness. Feel this pattern transforming your life by recalling a crisis you passed through such as a divorce, disease or financial loss. Notice the ways this loss loosened the principles you held to be true. After the event, remember how your Belief Grid would not return to its rigid categories. Within the ever-shifting currents of the Fluid Web, notice how the facts and opinions that worked on the solid ground of your Belief Grid no longer work in this watery world. Feel how you could move from constraining life to exploring its fluid possibilities.

10
LIFEBOAT

Pattern of Wisdom 10, Lifeboat illustrates the tendency to separate ourselves from the uncertainty of the Fluid Web. When the Belief Grid we create to protect ourselves from the divisions of the Primal Wound dissolves into a shimmering network of living, we often fear we will sink beneath the tides of change. Within the Fluid Web, shifting lines of measurement challenge our sense of order and safety. Yesterday a marriage was solid, today it crumbles in divorce. This week a job is secure, the next we are unemployed. Last month, spinach was a healthy food, now an outbreak of E. coli bacteria makes it unsafe to eat. Waves of change constantly form and reform in the ocean of living. In the Fluid Web, objects and beings are born only to decay and dissolve. Seasons pass, bodies age, friendships fade. To stay afloat, we create mental Lifeboats we believe will protect us from sinking in the unpredictable currents.

Zack, an award-winning furniture maker, used the pattern of the Lifeboat to respond to shifting circumstances in the following way. For 20 years, he was known in Chicago for creating high quality tables, chairs and other Arts and Crafts style items. Then a Swedish corporation opened a big box home decor outlet in town. They offered cut-rate prices and flooded the airwaves with ads promoting contemporary furniture. Zack's orders plunged. To stay afloat, he turned his woodworking skills to making kitchen cabinets for high-end custom homes.

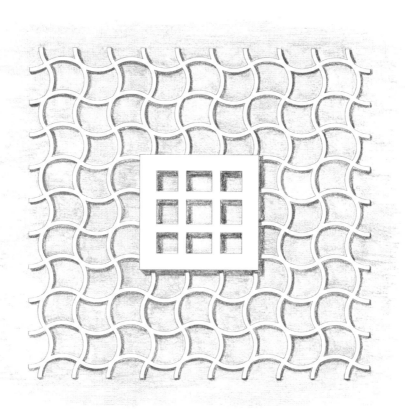

Pattern of Wisdom 10 • Lifeboat

To resist sinking beneath change, we try to separate ourselves from life.

This work was less artistic and called upon only a small percentage of the knowledge and skill he had developed over the years. Yet, it provided the Lifeboat he needed to navigate the changing market.

Zack's Lifeboat became his new reference point for surviving and thriving. He switched from a fine art oriented shop with two workers to an assembly line factory employing 25. Instead of crafting with loving detail, he turned to overall efficiency. Daily, he examined everything from the price of lumber to trucking costs and healthcare to determine if they strengthened or weakened his Lifeboat.

In another example of this pattern, Carol's Lifeboat was her reputation. She was a world-famous journalist known for honesty and integrity in exposing the truth. Then a source came to her with bad information about an insider trading scam. Hurrying to report the fraud, Carol neglected to check the facts she was given. The story turned out to be untrue. As a result, she was sued for libel and fired from her job. To keep her Lifeboat intact, she undertook measures to repair her reputation. First, she did a series of TV interviews admitting her wrong-doing and took complete responsibility for the false story. Then she dropped out of the public eye and let the negative reports about her fade. After six months of soul searching, she founded a watchdog group that checked the facts of news stories to reveal inaccuracies and distortions. She re-entered her profession with the Lifeboat of her reputation renewed and strengthened. From that time on, Carol screened every detail of every story she reported.

As we use the pattern our Lifeboats to screen what we meet in the Fluid Web, we solidify the distinct outlines of our personalities. What defines us also separates us from the currents of existence. While a Lifeboat's insulating walls shelter our sense of self, it also disconnects us from the revitalizing energy and wisdom flowing through the Fluid Web. It is like an American who tours Italy and only eats American-style fast food and sleeps in hotels filled with other Americans. Remaining in the familiar bubble of his Lifeboat, he misses the richness and delight of the local culture and cuisine.

The more clearly our Lifeboats separate us from the nurturing currents of the Fluid Web the more isolated we become. In time, our survival vessels can turn into self-made prisons. If maintaining the pattern of our disconnect becomes more important than receiving nourishment from the Fluid Web, we may become enclosed in lonely, alienating armor. As we suppress the tides of living, we may encase ourselves in a shell of anger, aloofness or depression.

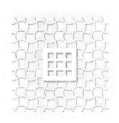 • *Sense your Lifeboat separating you from life.*
Pattern of Wisdom 10, Lifeboat depicts the structures we create to prevent drowning in the Fluid Web of existence. Experience this pattern in the qualities that define your personality from your profession and economic status through your family history and unique talents to your preferences about food and movies. Feel how what makes your Lifeboat unique also separates you from others. Sense how it limits where you go, who you interact with and what you do. With this in mind, experience your Lifeboat as a pattern of consciousness for navigating the Fluid Web.

11
CONTROL

Pattern of Wisdom 11, Control depicts the tendency to expand the protective powers of our Lifeboats. When we believe this pattern of consciousness is protecting us, its isolating and limiting effects can seem less important than maintaining its structure. Yet, riding our Lifeboats above the Fluid Web provides limited security. We remain vulnerable to the broader tides of change sweeping through the ocean of life. To increase personal safety, we often expand the reach of our Lifeboats, hoping to control wider and wider areas of the ever-shifting sea of existence.

We can act like settlers inhabiting a forested wilderness. First a few large trees are chopped down and used to build a cabin. Then an area around the cabin is cleared to plant gardens for a more stable food supply. After that, an even wider area of trees are cleared to establish a separation from forest fires. To further control the wilderness, the settlers block a stream with a dam and create a reservoir. They run pipes from the reservoir to the cabin to manage their water supply. Through the forest, they carve roads to receive raw materials and food from neighboring towns. The roads also let them bring their goods to market. Step by step, the settlers expand their territory of Control. They tame the unruly forces of nature to establish an orderly and predictable supply of food, shelter and clothing.

As changes in the Fluid Web rock the stability of our Lifeboats,

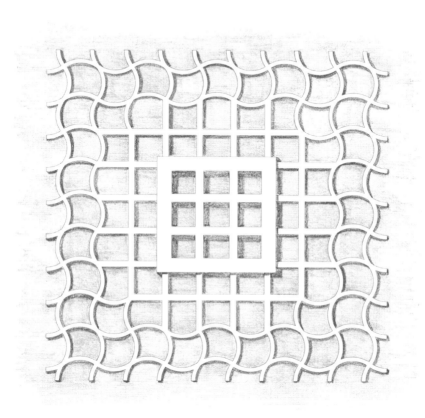

Pattern of Wisdom 11 • Control

To increase security, we try to suppress the tides of change.

we can falsely believe that problems would disappear if life would just stay put. We may think that if people only acted the way we wanted them to our lives would be safe and happy. With that purpose in mind, we may try to make the world conform to the principles and behaviors that make us feel secure. Through the pattern of Control, we attempt to press the currents of the Fluid Web into supply lines that feed our preferences for living. We see this behavior when a country invades territories rich in natural resources, when a business extends its reach across the globe, or a fanatical religious leader attempts to convert "unbelievers" to his faith.

Measures to increase Control can become excessive or costly, but we often ignore the price we pay to maintain them. Trying to manage

Through the pattern of Control, we try to turn waves of change into predictable conduits of supply.

irritating and threatening influences may cause us to push friends away, spend more money than we have, or work ourselves ragged. We may believe that suppressing actions are vital needs when they are merely personal preferences.

Consider the city planners in Oak Park, Michigan who threatened to put a woman in jail for growing a vegetable garden in her front yard. The codes controlling the city prohibited the planting of vegetables on the street side of her house, even if the plants were arranged in neatly ordered rows. Broccoli and roses are both plants, but the planning codes of Oak Park turned a preference for ornamental shrubs into a law.

The pattern of Control has its limits. Every person and event outside the reassuring lines of our Lifeboats can appear to be a threat. To avert these perceived dangers, we may try to turn everything within our field of influence into conduits of survival. As a result, we live in constant conflict with the shifting forces of life. Our days are spent trying to suppress one unruly event after another.

Our Lifeboats and the Fluid Web, however, are both patterns of consciousness. Lifeboats reveal the capacities of order and predictability. The Fluid Web displays the capacities of renewal and creativity. These two expressions only appear to fight one another. Orderliness cannot exist without renewal. The predictable will stagnate if it lacks creativity. As we navigate the ocean of existence, interactions between opposites make our journey come alive.

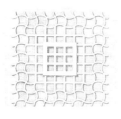

• *Feel your attempts to Control the world.*
Pattern of Wisdom 11, Control depicts efforts to expand the protection of our Lifeboats into our surroundings. In daily life, notice the ways you try to manage people and places to increase your sense of safety and security. Does this work or does life escape your attempts to tame it? Feel the struggle of trying to subdue the elusive currents of the Fluid Web. Sense Control as a pattern of consciousness helping you explore its possibilities.

12

BATTLEFIELD

Pattern of Wisdom 12, Battlefield illustrates further attempts to increase our security by dividing the Fluid Web into regions of safety and danger. We believe we can conquer the vast forces of existence by partitioning them into allies and enemies. Following this idea, we break the world into opposites—positive and negative, harmful and healthy, undermining and supportive, polluted and pure. The Fluid Web of existence becomes a checkerboard that differentiates desire from fear and wants from needs. Each person, action and relationship is zoned into areas of desirable or undesirable, success or failure, beautiful or ugly, sacred or profane. Every object and place is squeezed into one box or another. How we look, where we live, what we eat, and where we work are rated as to how they support or threaten our Lifeboats of survival.

Yet, trying to increase order by dividing the Fluid Web into different zones backfires. It generates chaos. The shifting terrain of our lives becomes a Battlefield of forces fighting for supremacy. What we want clashes with what we have. Where we long to be argues with where we are. Our desire for freedom quarrels with routines and responsibilities. Natural cycles of growth and decay become ongoing fights between good and evil. Rather than living the balanced, orderly life we imagined, we may come to believe that we must pass through an ongoing series of skirmishes.

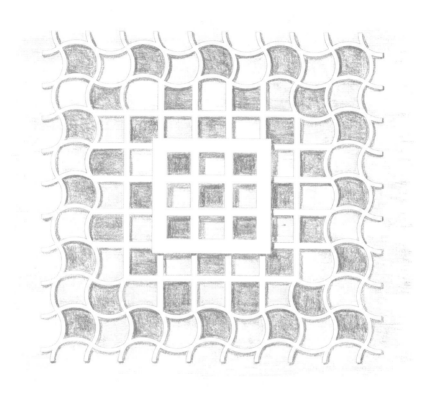

Pattern of Wisdom 12 • Battlefield

To deepen a sense of control, we divide life into zones of safety and danger.

The pattern of Battlefield consciousness was used by a minister named Derek. He believed that the local library should promote books on his faith and that those about other religions should be banned. With this purpose in mind, he mounted a campaign that preached his dividing views. This turned the local library into a Battlefield of warring ideas. The librarian fought back, arguing that readers should have open access to diverse beliefs. Derek became obsessed with combating and defeating the forces he believed were destroying his community. Strategies and tactics to overpower the "dangerous" books consumed him. When the librarian acquired a new series of volumes on world religions, Derek protested to the town council. The council meeting became a minefield of political forces. After an angry debate between people from different beliefs, the library was allowed to offer the new books. But tension and discord clouded the community.

Another example of the pattern of Battlefield consciousness occurred when a family in southern California put a children's swing set in the backyard of their suburban home. As soon as the play equipment was in place, neighbors began calling to ask when it was going to be removed. Other families in the neighborhood had put up swing sets with no problem. But, this one was placed within the view of neighbors who saw it as an eyesore. The children, on the other hand, loved their swing set and the creative fun it provided. The neighborhood became a Battlefield where some people fought for the rights of families to chose what they put in their backyards and others fought for what they believed was beautiful and would improve property values. Each side believed its position was vital to the good of the neighborhood and that they must win at any cost.

Surely there are genuine threats to our health and wellbeing. But, defining each person, place and event as an enemy or a friend divides life falsely. Doing so cuts us off from the nourishing influences that come from unexpected combinations of opposites. The immune system of our bodies is stronger if we grow up encountering some bacteria rather than living in a sterile environment. A forest would not be vitally alive if the forces of creation and destruction did not mix in numerous ways to nurture its creatures, plants and terrain. A musician may not develop her talent if she has never been challenged by difficult compositions. If, however, we persist in making strict separations between positive and negative powers, we turn our human journey into a miserable ordeal.

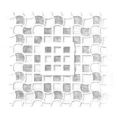

• *Sense zones of opposites igniting conflict.*

Pattern of Wisdom 12, Battlefield illustrates the conflicts we create by zoning our lives into a checkerboard of positive and negative forces. Experience this by drawing a grid on a piece of paper and shading it into a checkerboard. In the light squares, list the positive people, places and forces in your life. In the dark squares, write the negative ones. Feel the conflict created between the values in the light and dark squares. Study the positive values in the light squares and sense any negative values within them. Do the same with the dark squares. Look beyond the surface of the conflicting squares and see consciousness giving rise to both.

13

CONFUSION

Pattern of Wisdom 13, Confusion depicts the struggle between safety and danger throwing a Lifeboat into turmoil. When we make efforts to increase order and it produces chaos, the results can be baffling. We may not want to admit that attempting to control the Fluid Web ignites conflict. Instead, we often justify the fight, telling ourselves struggle is necessary to obtain what we need to survive. We continue to engage the battle and continue to knock our Lifeboats off balance. To keep our survival crafts afloat, we may blindly persist in pitting one part of life against another and keep churning the waters of conflict.

A business owner named Roger experienced the pattern of Confusion when he believed his company would be stronger if his employees fought each other for bonuses. His policies went beyond the normal incentives. He promoted an extreme level of competition that threw the business into Confusion. In subtle and obvious ways, he persisted in making his workplace a Battlefield. The self-made pressure cooker was agonizing. Stress and anxiety clouded the air. He pushed his employees to an emotional edge. Roger was not immune to the trauma he created. He suffered painful memories and distressing dreams. To avoid the pain, he avoided interacting with his staff. His memory became cloudy and his own work suffered. To deaden the ache of living between clashing forces, he numbed his emotions and detached himself from daily living. He drank too much at night

Pattern of Wisdom 13 • Confusion

Battles between safety and danger destabilize our survival structures.

and hid in his office much of the day. The conflict within him could only be restrained for so long before he erupted in anger and aggression. He barked at his employees and criticized them endlessly. In his highly sensitized state, he overreacted to the smallest irritation. Around him, everyone acted like they were tiptoeing on eggshells. He believed that this was the way of the world and the battle would continue without end. As a result, he became lost in Confusion.

Roger was locked in his Belief Grid. From this viewpoint, he assumed that repeating the same actions with greater effort would create balance. With more intensity, he pitted one employee against the other and the business became more destabilized. Roger ignored his business partner's reminder that insanity was doing the same thing over and over again and expecting a different result. Instead, he continued to enact the false belief that setting one part of the business against the other would create more growth.

When Roger's conflict-producing management style failed to produce progress, he blamed the turmoil on his partner, the employees and the economy. He denied his responsibility for the battle. Accusing others of undermining his business, however, made him feel powerless. Placing the fault for his confusion in the hands of others implied he did not have the strength to correct the situation. This transferred the wellbeing of his business to the mercy of forces outside himself. Any effort to restore balance seemed doomed to failure.

Being absorbed in struggle blinded Roger to what was still healthy in his business. His focus on the battle obscured the rich pool of talents within his employees. He overlooked the many ways their work kept the company on track. While he walked around in a cloud of conflict, he missed how their team spirit and skill made the day-to-day operations work. Despite Roger's attitude and actions, the employees were keeping the business afloat.

Confusion is consciousness twisted into conflict. It is like a rope tied in a knot. The way to remove a knot is not to tighten the rope. It is to loosen the tangle and return the rope to its original clarity. This may seem obvious. Yet, believing we live on a Battlefield confuses our vision. It is not essential that we use the patterns of the Lifeboat and the Battlefield to create the pattern of Confusion. Instead, we can sense these patterns as consciousness distorted by dividing life into zones of conflicting forces. Clarity returns not by trying harder to divide darkness from light, but by experiencing opposing forces as consciousness playing opposite roles to engage in a unified, dynamic dance.

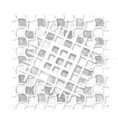

• *See conflicting opposites creating Confusion.* Pattern of Wisdom 13, Confusion depicts self-created conflicts between positive and negative values creating a muddle. Experience this pattern by noticing how setting values such as healthy and unhealthy or friendly and threatening against one another throws you off balance. Instead of viewing opposites as fighting, sense them dancing in dynamic harmony. Feel the clarity in an energetic flow of complementary forces.

14

DEFENSE

Pattern of Wisdom 14, Defense illustrates the tendency to armor ourselves against the self-created pattern of the Battlefield. Hunkering
down behind walls of ideals and beliefs, we may clutch whatever
system of economics, politics or spirituality that hardens the shell of
our Lifeboats. We further protect our survival craft by denying the
storms of conflict that jeopardize the rightness of our viewpoints. Re-
peatedly, we may reject the shocking realization that we sabotage ourselves by dividing the Fluid Web of life into the pattern of a Battlefield.
Responding defensively, we may shield ourselves against unwanted
intrusions from people and events. A silent "No" can become our first
response to every situation.

Roger defended his Lifeboat by continuing to promote his conflict-producing management style. His business partner took him
aside and explained how his attitude and actions were undermining
their company. Roger refused to listen. Instead, he found scientific
studies proving that employees performed better when they compet-
ed for financial rewards. To manipulate office politics toward his view,
he covertly promised three of his most eager employees bigger bonuses, promotions and company cars if they intensified their aggres-
sive behavior. As a result, the mood in the company darkened further.
His partner continued to protest, barging into Roger's office waving
reports showing how their profits were plummeting. Roger rejected

Pattern of Wisdom 14 • Defense

To guard against confusion, we fortify our lives with separating walls.

each complaint without listening. Being right had become more important to him than the wellbeing of his business and his employees.

Hidden behind the protecting walls of his Lifeboat of beliefs, anxiety flooded him. To cope with the stress, he deadened his mind with anger and alcohol. Secretly, he sank into despair. Hoping to think his way out of the situation, he devised detailed explanations about the ways his partner, his employees and rival firms endangered his business. To maintain his defensive posture, he surrounded himself with books and movies reinforcing the stance that aggression and infighting strengthened productivity.

The battle within the company raged on. Profits continued to drop. When the clashes he had ignited did not stop and the plummeting profits threatened to sweep his company into bankruptcy, Roger became enraged. He launched a takeover attack against his business partner and fired twenty percent of his staff, sending shock waves of fear through his remaining employees. Attempting to guard his business, Roger used neurotic tactics that undermined everything he had worked for.

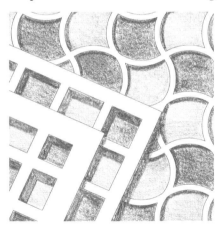

We must protect ourselves from real danger, but building a fortress against life disconnects us from the nourishing and renewing forces of change.

Defensive walls such as those Roger created came from

misunderstanding what it is to be safe within consciousness. We often believe that security results from pushing things away or striking out at threats. Rejecting life, however, only restarts the conflict that put us in danger in the first place. Hazards and resistance to them are patterns of consciousness. Since we are consciousness too, we cannot push away what we are. As it turns out, the best defense against this type of danger is letting go of patterns of conflict within ourselves.

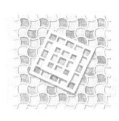

• *Sense Defenses creating conflict.*

Pattern of Wisdom 14, Defense illustrates how we use beliefs to armor ourselves against the self-created pattern of the Battlefield. Experience this when you feel threatened by conflict. Notice if you respond to friction by denying the self-generated threat exists. Even though the conflict of the Battlefield stems from a self-created pattern, do you look for evidence of threats from outside yourself to validate your resistance? Notice if your defenses ignite more conflict. Is a silent "No" your response to this situation? Despite self-armoring behavior, are you still anxious? In response to anxiety, do you try to numb yourself? If conflict continues, does your frustration turn into defensive anger? To loosen the grip of this pattern, sense the patterns of the Battlefield and Control as designs of consciousness expressing the coexistence of movement and stillness, conflict and harmony, chaos and calm and other opposites.

15

FLOOD

Pattern of Wisdom 15, Flood illustrates how, despite our defenses, the Lifeboats securing our sense of wellbeing are eventually overpowered by a crisis such as disease, divorce or financial loss. The battling waves of opposites—friends and enemies, goods and evils—inundate our frameworks of order. Swirling currents dissolve the clear descriptions of who we are, why we are here and where we are going.

Bella believed she maintained perfect health until the pattern of the Flood changed all that. She ate only fresh, organic, vegetarian meals. Every morning she did 30 minutes of meditation and 45 minutes of yoga before bicycling to work. She looked for the positive side of everything and did whatever she could to create loving relationships. When Bella's doctor told her she had breast cancer, the diagnosis flooded her mind. The belief that a healthy lifestyle would ward off disease was swept from the core of her life. She felt washed out to sea. With her Belief Grid gone, she found nothing to cling to. The sheltering port of good food, exercise and friendship no longer offered protection from the disease that had overtaken her body. The fortified walls defending her Lifeboat dissolved. The categories she had used to separate safety from danger no longer boxed her life into distinct parts. Dividing the Fluid Web into opposites no longer described her experience. Words that separated gain from loss, love from resistance and friend from enemy did not communicate the emerging both/and

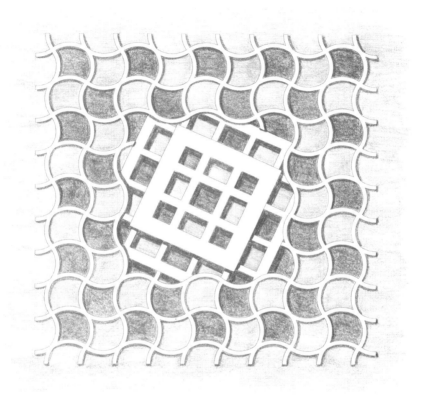

Pattern of Wisdom 15 • Flood

Despite strong defenses, our lives are overwhelmed by tides of change.

experience of life swirling around her. The values she had relied upon for security and predictability were swept into tidal flows of living. It became impossible for her to clearly divide the forces of health from the forces of destruction threatening her with death.

Despite the cancer flooding her life, Bella struggled to keep her healthy lifestyle afloat. As the undertow of forces dragged her from the belief that she was in complete control of her life, she acknowledged the currents of consciousness that connected her to the wider world. Yet, as cancer carried her from the life she knew, she still reached for the belief that the right diet, meditation and exercise

Our defenses are no match for the vast forces sweeping through the ocean of existence.

would conquer the disease. She found articles about women who had cured themselves of cancer naturally and followed the regimen that had worked for them. Grasping at bits of hope, she courageously took intensive combinations of herbs and vitamins. She clung to her identity as a person of glowing fitness. Determined, she increased her time on the meditation cushion and the yoga mat. She undertook juice fasts and colon cleanses. To increase her positive mood, she amped up her loving behavior and doubled her hours helping out at the local food bank. Clinging to her beliefs, she refused the chemotherapy and mastectomy her doctor advocated, shutting out these possible options for recovery. Despite her valiant efforts, the cancer spread to her lymph nodes. Bella sensed herself sinking beneath the flood of disease overwhelming her.

There is no denying the devastating impact of a Flood. We are better able to survive it, however, when we experience both our Lifeboats and the waves swamping them as patterns of consciousness sweeping over itself. The rigid lines of our survival rafts and the waves of energy they ride are both animated by the same life force. Our patterns of living are not annihilated. They are pulled beyond personal preferences into new patterns and new possibilities.

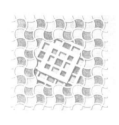

• Feel the Flood swamping your Lifeboat.
Pattern of Wisdom 15, Flood illustrates a crisis overwhelming a Lifeboat. We experience this pattern of consciousness when we are overtaken by a disease, a divorce, an economic collapse or a natural disaster. To sense the effects of the Flood, recall a time when a crisis swept through your life. Did you respond by struggling to stay afloat? Despite your best efforts, did forces beyond your control overwhelm you? What did you feel when sinking beneath the waves of the event? While the loss was happening, did you discover strengths and knowledge that remained? Without denying the impact of the Flood, see both your Lifeboat and the waves swamping it as a pattern of shimmering consciousness sweeping through you into itself. Instead of sensing the flood as a loss, experience it as a wave rolling through one unbroken ocean of existence.

16

SURRENDER

Pattern of Wisdom 16, Surrender depicts the dissolving of emotional blocks and attitudes that isolate us from the rest of life. A sinking Lifeboat does not drown us. When we release our protective armor, we can rediscover our kinship with fluid consciousness. As we swim with the currents of the Fluid Web the divisions that ignited conflict and suffering subside. We see that clashing people and places only appeared to be separate. Rather, they are interconnected waves rising and falling within one shimmering sea of energy and wisdom. What seemed to be forces competing for domination can now be engaged as multi-dimensional flows of consciousness. Within this awakening, we move away from perceiving our individual, separate selves as the central reason for living and the source of action. The tides of life carry us toward acknowledging that we are countless waveforms within a vast ocean of consciousness.

Bella had used the pattern of the Lifeboat to separate her body from the swirling currents of cancer and the negative side-effects of medical treatment. When alternative methods for healing did not stop the disease, she surrendered to the chemotherapy and surgery her doctor recommended. After spending years eating chemical-free food, the thought of toxic drugs flowing through her veins terrified her. Since diet and exercise had strengthened her body in health, she thought it could lessen the damaging effects of the chemotherapy.

Pattern of Wisdom 16 • Surrender

Yielding to tides of change, we become attuned to the currents of living.

Facing the choice between clinging to her beliefs or freeing herself from cancer, she realized that giving in did not mean she was giving up. She turned her passion for health toward learning everything about her therapy. Eating the right foods and doing purifying yoga positions fortified her through the rocky days of chemotherapy.

By yielding to the shifting currents of life, Bella lessened her fears and called forth her strengths. To her surprise, the doctors and nurses who administered her treatment were loving and gentle. Opening to their care dissolved the isolation of fighting the disease alone. It allowed her to be supported by the strengths of others. As a result, her limited power to deal with cancer expanded to include the vaster forces flowing through the Fluid Web of existence.

In the process, Bella discovered that the intense routine of diet and exercise that had defined her had also disguised an underlying fear of life. What had looked like an embrace of health had been a defense against the vast powers of living. In the process of surrendering to the treatments for a life-threatening disease, she found that her vitality and joy were not to be found in her defenses. They were in the energy and wisdom accessed by dissolving them. The Flood that had overwhelmed her also transformed her. The Lifeboat of defense became a vessel for sailing the ocean of existence. Where she had previously resisted the ebb and flow of change, she now looked for shifting paths of transformation. Where she had opposed the forces that challenged her beliefs, she now opened her mind and body to receive nurturing guidance and encouragement from them. What had been clashing forces threatening to destroy her became revitalizing energies that carried her through unfolding mysteries. In *Surrender*, she turned what appeared to be her greatest loss into a gain beyond her imagination.

Bella summarized the process of surrender that opened her to a richer experience of living in the following way: 1) She acknowledged the flood of forces dissolving the pattern of her Lifeboat. 2) Within the pain and grief of losing her vessel of supporting beliefs, she accepted that her Lifeboat pattern had dissolved. 3) Without the vessel of her supporting beliefs, she saw the strengths and knowledge that had held her Lifeboat pattern together. 4) With these strengths and knowledge, she engaged the greater flow of life. 5) Responding to shifting events in this way, she experienced her individuality as a wave on the ocean of consciousness. 6) She sensed this wave as the pattern of the Fluid Web of life interacting with itself through her. 7) When she encountered challenges, this more fluid and connected experience of the world allowed her to deal with obstacles and move ahead with greater freedom.

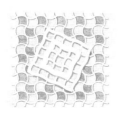

• *Sense Surrender in the flow of existence.*
Pattern of Wisdom 16, Surrender depicts surviving a crisis and rediscovering our kinship with the Fluid Web of existence. To experience this pattern, recall a time when you survived a turning point in your life. If you were overwhelmed by the event, follow Bella's summary of the seven stages of Surrender described above and notice what happens.

17

DIALOGUE

Pattern of Wisdom 17, Dialogue depicts inhabiting the Fluid Web as an ongoing conversation with the currents of consciousness. As we navigate the human journey, daily life can become an ongoing interchange with the waves of existence. Each encounter expands beyond an interaction between one isolated person and another. Our lives enter a fluid experience of consciousness speaking with itself through each individual. We open to experiencing energy and intelligence permeating every place and event. The passing joys and pains of work and play become infused with a continuum of wisdom. Each wave in the ocean of living can be engaged as a pattern of fluid consciousness.

Bella found that opening to the flowing unity of living did not dissolve her individual viewpoint. She still preferred running shoes to high heels, vegetables to steak, and progressive politicians to conservatives. Yet, she did not cling to a single perspective. She willingly moved from one position to another to act in harmony with the forces and forms that life called forth at any given moment. One day, a disagreement with a friend was resolved by Bella taking a flexible attitude and accepting what was outside her personal preferences. Another day, a political debate required a clear position that supported one side of an issue over another. All the while, she looked through separate viewpoints to the one consciousness permeating all viewpoints. Behind diverse intentions and actions, she experienced

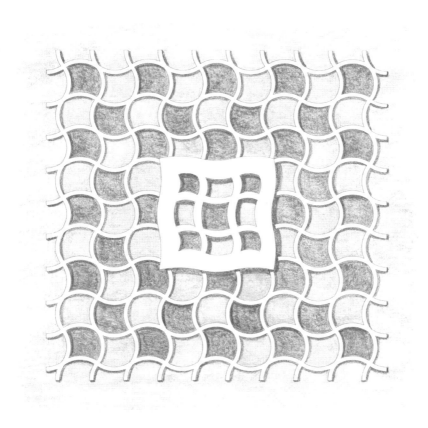

Pattern of Wisdom 17 • Dialogue

Aligned with currents of consciousness, life becomes a conversation of discovery.

a shared search for freedom and happiness. Opposing perspectives were no longer seen as competing for domination. She sensed them as life wrestling with itself to reveal the most useful options.

Through this experience, Bella let go of defining herself by her hopes and fears, pleasures and pains, gains and losses. Instead, she accepted and supported her indefinable nature. Her personal aspirations widened to include the tides of consciousness expressing itself through varied personalities. In turn, she experienced consciousness as assuming and releasing an endless series of identities and appearances. Walking through a forest one day, she sensed the ecosystem forming and reforming itself through the variety of plants and animals being born, living and dying within it. She saw the earth giving rise to plants, then plants feeding animals, then one animal swallowing another, then animals being devoured by the earth. In the ocean of continuous change, she discovered each individual wave of existence rising from the dissolution of a previous wave.

Life carried Bella into the experience of consciousness permeating everything. Fragmented perceptions could no longer obscure her connection to life's deeper realities. She could not escape the unity of living because she was one with that unity. Even if she attempted to flee the mysterious paradoxes of life, her escape routes dissolved into elusive currents of consciousness. She surrendered more deeply to life and accepted her personal actions as expressions of the impersonal consciousness permeating the world. Beyond intellectual comprehension, she embraced her role in the mysterious horrors and wonders through which life consumed itself to regenerate itself.

By realizing that she embodied the fluid forces of living, Bella no longer attempted to freeze time and control change. Instead of straining to maintain what already existed, she willingly played her part in opening the way to fresh creation after fresh creation. She no longer feared that the next event would destroy her life. Instead, she engaged each moment as a pattern of consciousness shimmering through transformation after transformation, a dialogue of discovering possibility after possibility.

• *Experience life as an ongoing conversation.*
Pattern of Wisdom 17, Dialogue illustrates dwelling in the Fluid Web as an ongoing conversation with the currents of consciousness. Experience this in daily life by sensing each person, place and event as a wave of consciousness in the ocean of existence. Sense each wave rising from the dissolution of previous waves. Feel your thoughts and actions as expressions of a wider network of flowing energy and intelligence. Instead of trying to capture life in fixed moments, open to playing your role in facilitating unending tides of change. Experience every interaction as a pattern of consciousness speaking with itself through you. Sense yourself as a pattern of consciousness arising from the broader pattern of the Fluid Web.

18

VIEW FIELD

Pattern of Wisdom 18, View Field illustrates the process of consciousness carrying us from the center of attention to expanded visions of life. As infants we may stand at the core of family attention. Then, going to school takes us into a field of other students. Entering the workforce, in turn, opens to a wider field of humanity. In this way, our centralized viewpoints broaden to include the expanded vision of View Fields. We move out of experiencing the world through a single standpoint to experiencing it from wider expanses of awareness. Individual perspectives stretch to function from fields of multidimensional seeing. We grow from sensing ourselves as separate individuals to

acting from broader fields of consciousness.

Our experience shifts from a centralized viewpoint to a broad View Field of perception.

In his work as a gardener, Bill discovered the power of opening from viewpoint to viewpoint and discovering wider and wider View Fields of experience. Because of the depressed economy, he started a vegetable garden on an abandoned lot next to his house. He made the tiny plot as fertile as possible and planted foods that grew well in the city's microclimate. When his neighbors saw the abundance of flourishing vegetables, they

Pattern of Wisdom 18 • View Field

Shifting viewpoints expand personal concerns into View Fields of shared discovery.

asked Bill to teach them his secrets. Not having finished high school, he was unsure he could teach anybody anything. But he looked beyond the needs of his own garden and taught his neighbors what he knew. Soon the entire vacant lot was covered with thriving gardens and people were harvesting an abundance of organic produce. A local television station heard of the success and broadcast a story on the evening news. When the mayor learned about the derelict lot that had been turned into burgeoning gardens, he asked Bill to give classes at the city's high schools. The task seemed daunting, but Bill stepped beyond his comfort zone and worked with the students throughout the town. At each high school, he encountered different soil conditions and students from different social and economic backgrounds. To meet the challenge, he enlarged his understanding of enriching and balancing varied soil conditions. He also broadened his abilities to inspire students from different circumstances. Soon, the governor enlisted Bill to travel statewide and share his expanding knowledge. Now he had to learn about the plants and techniques that would work in the varied microclimates of the state. Each shift from a smaller to a wider community was a shift of viewpoint. With each shift of viewpoint, his life stretched to a greater View Field.

Looking back on his unexpected journey, Bill saw the shifting viewpoints of his path had followed a spiral arc. His individual attention had pivoted on one event, then had spun onward to the next. Each time he released one viewpoint and expanded to a wider View Field, a worn out layer of knowledge and experience had fallen away to reveal a new one. Like a snake shedding old skin, each release of

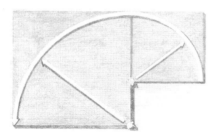

Shifting viewpoints and widening View Fields trace spiral paths of discovery.

limited, personal awareness had uncovered a new layer of expanded, collective consciousness. He noticed that his spiraling journey had no conscious beginning. He had no idea where it would end. Yet, the coiling path wove each of Bill's experiences into the broader continuum of his life.

This thread of perception revealed that each event on his life journey appeared to be separate and disconnected. Yet, it had unfolded along a continuous plot line. The arc of his story had traveled a specific path, but it eluded precise measurement. Inches could not determine the dimensions of his changing viewpoints. Minutes could not mark the time it took to travel from one insight to another.

• *Sense viewpoints expanding into View Fields.*
Pattern 18, View Field illustrates the path of consciousness carrying us from the center of attention to expanded visions of life. Experience this by imagining: 1) the arrows in the drawing as rays of perception 2) the arcs as sweeps of perception 3) the pivot points of the rays of perception as different viewpoints and 4) the series of squares as widening View Fields of perception. Feel the arc of your consciousness moving from viewpoint to viewpoint and opening to wider and wider View Fields of life.

19

GROWTH–DECAY–RENEWAL

Pattern of Wisdom 19, Growth–Decay–Renewal depicts how the shifting viewpoints that generate spirals of growth also generate spirals of decay, fostering renewal. In the process, arcs of rising hope meet arcs of sinking doubt. Confusion swirls about clarity. Joy and sorrow circle one another. These opposing arcs ignite a charged space between them. Within this lively opening, potential energy and knowledge swirl into thoughts and actions. Formless consciousness rolls into creative visions. Silent awareness stirs into stories and music.

Marta found the charged opening between arcs of growth and decay by working with her family's building supply business. After three generations of selling high quality lumber, wood flooring and stone pavers, she wanted to move their products in a more ecological direction. To do so, she studied the processes of nature. Surprisingly, she found a paradox in ecology—imbalance produced balanced ebbs and flows of nourishment. Rhythms of interaction between the opposites of birth and death renewed life again and again. Contrasting arcs of winter and summer, frost and heat, revolved around each other to revitalize soil and water, plants and animals. The waxing and waning of light/dark, heat/cold, dry/moist and other contrasting pairs restored the earth through currents of dynamic balance. Arcs of conception and growth were counterbalanced by arcs of decay and death. These rounds of development and dissolution were not in conflict.

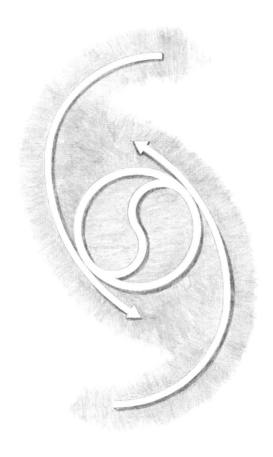

Pattern of Wisdom 19 • Growth–Decay–Renewal

Imbalance cycles consciousness into dynamic balance.

They embodied an alternating continuity of change.

Marta also learned that the ebb and flow of spiraling growth occurred within a single loop of life renewing itself. Through continuous cycles of self-fertilization the earth regenerated its energies and patterns of living. A wetland ecosystem, for example, revitalized itself through the rhythms of plants sprouting, growing, decaying and sprouting again. Each union of opposites created and recreated an eternal marriage of nature with itself.

Embracing the seeming contradictions of nature, Marta expanded the family business into selling salvaged building materials. Sections of her city were littered with derelict houses. Where others saw a decaying wasteland, she saw fertile ground for new growth. The owners of the crumbling houses were happy to free their land of useless blight. In turn, Marta's customers were delighted to buy redwood siding, oak flooring and cobblestone pavers with colors and textures that had deepened with age.

Through this dynamic, Marta connected change to completeness. Dismantling the old buildings and reassembling the materials in new houses were not separate ends and beginnings. They were phases in one, continuous process of decay and renewal. Marta related it to the shaping and reshaping of ocean waves that did not alter the completeness of the ocean. Salvaging old materials reflected nature's ecology. It participated in the rounds of life consuming and digesting itself again and again without fracturing its wholeness. The salvage business opened the way for Marta to see the energy and intelligence of nature moving through changing physical forms. The continuous transformations of creation revealed an unbroken unity.

To access the wisdom of Growth–Decay–Renewal, life calls us to experience the mystery of dissolution giving rise to birth. To be in harmony with this paradox is to sense decline as a phase in a continuous cycle of renewal. It is a contradiction that goes against the gut instinct that wellbeing is maintained through static balance. In reality, imbalance turns the wheel of life, rotating it through increase, decrease and regeneration. Imbalance and balance, growth and decay may appear to be in conflict, but they are in harmony. Blossoming and withering revolve about one another to enliven a dynamic space beyond balance and imbalance. Accessing this indescribable, yet vital, core is the wisdom of living a deeper level of renewal, one that is entered through patterns of change while being unaffected by change.

• *Experience imbalance generating balance.*
Pattern of Wisdom 19, Growth–Decay–Renewal depicts how the shifting viewpoints that generate spirals of growth also generate spirals of decay, fostering renewal. To feel this pattern moving through your life, notice the thoughts in your mind arising, fading and returning. Experience relationships sparking, dimming and re-igniting. Watch finances increasing, decreasing and increasing again. Feel the paradox of decay leading to renewal. Sense the charged space this cycle generates at the core of your life. Feel the deeper renewal of this charged space. Experience imbalance regenerating balance.

20
LABYRINTH

Pattern of Wisdom 20, Labyrinth depicts the arcs of birth and decay that generate renewal also bending our human journey into a convoluted path. In this process, our attempts to achieve specific goals fold into twisting, turning delays and discoveries. A simple plan to lose a few pounds, for example, can turn into an elaborate excursion through the effects of diet and exercise. Desires for quick, clear answers about life can veer into an ongoing journey through ancient wisdom teachings and arcane mysteries. An innocent inquiry into the meaning of a dream can lead to immersion in the study of psychological complexes. The overview of a healthcare plan can descend into a confusing tangle of hidden costs and pitfalls. Through these twists and turns, the broad vision of View Fields becomes the knotted consciousness of Labyrinths. And like wandering the streets of a medieval city reveals the town's intimate sounds and colors, wending our way through the creases of human experience brings us into intimate contact with more detailed qualities and forms of consciousness.

Connor, an author of mystery novels, saw the plots of his stories as complex labyrinths. The power of his books grew from the challenges his characters faced. His plots took his heroes and villains through disorienting paths and blind passages. This allowed him to bring forth the deeper strengths and knowledge of each personality. Placing obstacle after obstacle along the winding story lines intensified the plot

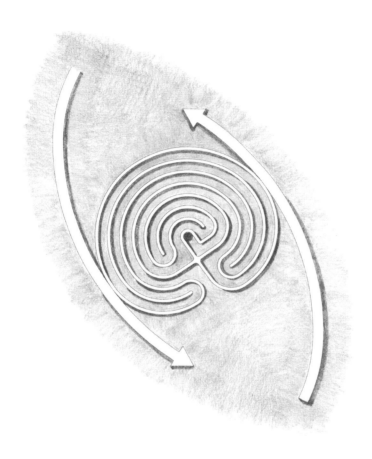

Pattern of Wisdom 20 • Labyrinth

Counterbalancing forces bend our lives into winding paths of discovery.

and captured the attention of his readers. As his characters battled forces of oppression, followed the passions of love, or made scientific breakthroughs, they collided with obstacle after obstacle. The suspense in the story mounted. Each encounter with resistance opened a gap between a character's desires and her achievements. It divulged the differences between her intentions and the outcomes. The gaps between expectations and results appeared to be empty spaces or clouds of unknowing. Yet, to get what she wanted, the character had to risk passing through the unknown. By entering unfamiliar territory she discovered hidden powers and wisdom.

As Connor's characters passed through unfamiliar spaces again and again, each step of a plot became an initiation into deeper riddles of human experience. Crossing each threshold offered a breakthrough into another obscure place and revealed more intimate connections with the subtler mysteries of living. Traveling through fold after fold of these Labyrinths rubbed away the assumptions and expectations that obscured a character's vision of how her story would reveal itself. At the beginning of the novel, each character was filled with ideas about who she was and what the world could be. She overflowed with preconceptions about love, wisdom, power, freedom and success. The story's convoluted passage through the Labyrinth stripped away her false ideas to reveal lasting truths.

If a character resisted the twists and turns of the plot or tried to straighten its path, he ensnared himself more deeply in the opposing forces of the story. The character moved from exploring life's possibilities to attempting to escape its narrowing restrictions. If he denied the forces confronting him, the smooth arc of his journey was distorted into a fearful jumble of blind passages. The more he struggled to unravel the knotted path, the more ensnared he became.

By willingly entering the Labyrinth of Connor's stories, readers discovered that the twists and turns of the plot were not physical obstacles. They were patterns of energy and wisdom supporting and guiding the storyline. Passing through fears, his characters found hope. Meandering through the world, they discovered themselves. Traveling alone revealed their connections to the rest of life.

 **• *Experience the passage through the Labyrinth.*** Pattern of Wisdom 20, Labyrinth depicts the arcs of birth and decay that generate renewal also bending the human journey into a convoluted path. To feel the opposing arcs of growth and decay generate the twists and turns of the labyrinth, sense how your life journey is less like a straight line and more like a winding path. Feel the challenges you encounter on your curving trail. Notice how actions that bring an unwanted reaction open a gap between expectation and result. Within these gaps, discover deeper strengths and knowledge. Sense how passing through the labyrinth of your life wears away false ideas and reveals what is unworkable in your actions. Instead of experiencing your winding path as strewn with obstacles, sense it as a pattern of consciousness supporting and guiding your way.

21
WORDLESS WISDOM

Pattern 21, Wordless Wisdom illustrates the twisting, turning journey of the Labyrinth leading to an unexpected core of knowledge. On the winding trail guiding us to the heart of the human quest, we gain wisdom about ourselves and the world that can be described. When we reach the end of descriptions, we enter transcendent wisdom that is beyond words. We encounter what seems to be emptiness, a chasm devoid of knowledge. Yet, this transcendent core has a presence and sense of knowing that our minds cannot process. No matter how much we would like the space of this invisible wisdom to show itself in physical form, it remains invisible. Attempts to describe this inexpressible wisdom vanish as immediately as writing words on the wind. Efforts to shape this immeasurable knowingness into measurable categories of knowledge disappear as instantly as sculptures carved in flowing water.

Connor organized the plots of his novels to lead readers to ah-ha moments of Wordless Wisdom. The hopes and fears, deaths and discoveries, gains and losses his characters passed through were preparation for the breathless climax of the book. The actions and emotions that he could describe were setups for what he could not put into words. The knowledge that assisted the characters in navigating the logical achievements of their journey all pointed to a knowingness that did not rely on the logic of achievement. This knowingness did

Pattern of Wisdom 21 • Wordless Wisdom

The twists and turns of living lead to indescribable knowledge.

not come from the proof of the senses or the authority of scientists and sages. It came from the story opening to the direct experience of consciousness unconditioned by thoughts, words or actions. Connor gauged the success of a book by whether or not it evoked that transcendent moment.

In similar ways, our own lives can open to Wordless Wisdom. We can enter it during meditation, a yoga session or a walk through a beautiful place. Transcendent knowledge can also appear in the midst of creative work, a traffic jam or a comedy movie. This mysterious realization can be short-lived, however. Often, we cling to the ideas and experiences that brought us to an encounter with Wordless Wisdom. We hang onto the forms of contemplation, styles of compassionate action and methods of inspiring creativity that opened the way to transcendent vitality. We act like a man who confuses the ocean with the automobile that carried him to the shore. Wordless Wisdom can be confused with the words and actions that awaken us to it. Because of this, we can remain struck in the belief that only facts prove the usefulness of a transcendent experience. We may think that if Wordless Wisdom cannot be measured by scientific formulas it does not exist or has no value.

If we resist Wordless Wisdom in these ways, we extend our journey through the Labyrinth of obstacles. Again and again rational modes of perceiving, acting and achieving reach a transcendent space. Logic dissolves into Wordless Wisdom. Ignoring this realization again and again sends us back through the snaking passage. Eventually, we learn to travel the ongoing sequences of individual dissolutions and renewals without losing the awareness of the Wordless Wisdom at the core. We can come to see that every movement occurs in reference to transcendent knowledge. Then, we experience sounds resonating within silence and forms coming alive in relationship to space. As the poet Robert Frost wrote: "We dance around the ring and suppose. The secret sits in the middle and knows."

• *Acknowledge the effects of Wordless Wisdom.* Pattern of Wisdom 21, Wordless Wisdom illustrates the inexpressible knowledge found at the core of the Labyrinth. To experience the arcing lines of the Labyrinth framing this transcendent consciousness, recall moments when you experienced a knowingness that could not be described. Feel the ways this Wordless Wisdom influenced you. Were you filled with lively peace? Did your surroundings come alive with an inner glow? When the experience faded, were there ways you denied your contact with Wordless Wisdom? Did resistance to, or doubt about, Wordless Wisdom send you back to a twisting, turning path of challenges and realizations? Did passing through change after change and encountering Wordless Wisdom again and again reveal the consciousness that did not change? As you pass through the challenges of your day, notice the gaps, however slight, that reveal Wordless Wisdom. Instead of discounting the gaps as useless breaks, open to their calm vitality. Savor the quiet connection to life and silent knowingness these gaps provide. Receive Wordless Wisdom as a nurturing force.

22

FLOWERING

Pattern of Wisdom 22, Flowering depicts the blossoming of totality on the human journey. As we experience the silent consciousness of Wordless Wisdom coupled with the active consciousness of the Labyrinth's path, the complete range of life's possibilities opens before us. Inhabiting both realities, we no longer encounter each impulse of life as an isolated event. Instead we can cooperate with the integrated flow of energy and wisdom coursing through our veins. Worries about controlling the outcome of each situation can be loosened. We can collaborate with the ongoing, interconnected flow of creation.

A painter named Lena used the combination of silent and active consciousness as a guiding theme in her work. One of her most famous pictures used this motif to explore the hidden dialogue between security and adventure. On the one hand, the painting employed the stable forms of squares and rectangles to represent the desire to maintain a predictable and familiar supply of food, shelter and loving support. On the other hand, she used wavy lines, spirals and other fluid forms to express the energies of life wanting to grow and break the boredom of tedious patterns and routines. On the backdrop of stability, she depicted the longing for new friends, foreign travel, exotic foods and exciting stories. Her painting also described the desire for delightful surprises and visions inspired by dreams.

At the center of the painting, Lena portrayed the friction between

Pattern of Wisdom 22 • Flowering

Wordless Wisdom blossoms in radiant patterns of consciousness.

the desire for security and the desire for adventure. With bright crimson and green she showed a seed of totality bursting toward expansion. Vermilion and cobalt blue depicted the life force exploding through a circle of present conditions and growing toward new experiences and capacities. From there, each shoot of growth followed its own cycle of development, decay and renewal. Then she showed the impulses of life spreading shoots of possibility in every direction.

To describe the ways consciousness explores totality, Lena included roots plunging into a dense, obscure underworld of primal instinct, murky compulsions and soulful connections. She showed consciousness rising toward vast, clear spaces to explore the sky world of rational intellect, aspirations and spiritual freedom. Between the underworld and sky-world, her painting cycled through the day world of routine patterns, explainable motives and conventional relationships. Layering ring upon ring, she depicted the totality of consciousness growing through itself toward the full flowering of life.

In the process of painting the spreading rings of her design, Lena let go of creating from her thinking mind. Instead, she allowed the radiant geometries to flow through her brushstrokes spontaneously. To her surprise, the patterns that appeared were precise and complete. The order of her flowering forms delighted her desire for structure while taking her beyond preconceived frameworks of design. Her painting came alive with unexpected combinations of vivid colors and lush textures. The patterns in her work spontaneously reflected the configurations of flowers, crystals, animals, galaxies and other forms in nature. The harmony of elements within Lena's work offered a vision of the universe in miniature. The microcosm she created showed the map through which the possibilities of life flower.

Lena's painting depicted the totality of consciousness Flowering within us. It revealed our coexisting desires for safety and adventure and the ways these opposing longings urge us to look for resolution. Her images portrayed this search traveling through secrets and basic urges, far-reaching plans and inspired visions, concrete programs and mundane schedules. Her work illustrated this totality Flowering in patterns that reflected the instinctual, organic designs of nature.

As consciousness flowers, our lives reflect the patterns of nature.

• Sense the blossoming of totality in daily life.
Pattern 22, Flowering depicts the flourishing of wisdom on the human journey. Experience this by recalling a time of radiant inspiration such as a loving moment or a creative breakthrough. During this glowing moment, did you feel that everything fell into place and you were connecting to the rest of life? Did you sense a unity between the radiance within yourself and the radiance within the world. Savor the beauty and aliveness of this Flowering pattern of consciousness.

23
RELEASE

Pattern of Wisdom 23, Release illustrates letting go of cherished experiences to reveal new inspirations and realizations. The Flowering of consciousness can feel so wonderful that we want to freeze-frame the experience. Hoping to prevent the glow from slipping away, we may try to hold consciousness in a fixed state. Life, however, creates a vital form, not for the sake of that form, but to facilitate openings to deeper and deeper levels of radiance. A tree, for example, does not generate branches, leaves and flowers for their own ends. These physical forms serve as vehicles for energy and wisdom to shape and dissolve the tree in cycles of renewal. Paradoxically, releasing the radiant flowering of consciousness allows our human journey to blossom in riper fruits of consciousness. Like a plum tree losing its flowers in spring to make way for summer fruit, life calls us to release the brilliant blossoming of consciousness and open the way to richer, more expansive dimensions of experience.

This wisdom is expressed in the Tibetan tradition of making circular designs of the universe with colored sand. In this ancient ceremony, these complex designs, called mandalas, are created by laying down the brightly tinted sand grain by grain. It takes four Buddhist monks working together for many days to complete the intricate patterns. Creating these beautiful and elaborate mandalas is only the first phase of the ceremony. Dismantling them is given equal importance.

Pattern of Wisdom 23 • Release

Letting go of cherished experiences frees us to enter deeper possibilities of living.

With ritual attention, the mandalas are disassembled in a prescribed order. Then the monks sweep the colored sand into an urn. The urn is wrapped in silk and carried to a river. At the riverbank, the sand from the mandala is poured into the flowing water. In this way, the glorious, sacred design is released forever. It cannot be frozen in time or reconstituted in any place.

Maggie, an aging actress, saw the ceremony of creating and releasing the sand mandala as a reflection of her life experience. Looking back on her human journey, she imagined the people and places she had encountered as being within a vast circle. The achievements and adventures in her life mandala had gathered day by day, experience by experience. What made relationships and events come alive, however, was not clinging to her life as a fixed object. The comings and goings of family and friends had filled her days with life. By passing through childhood and adulthood, through college and career, through home and the world, and releasing each of these physical forms, she came to know the formless consciousness animating her. In losing each shape of living, she discovered the consciousness that did not come and go, but continued through any change.

Just as the monks willingly poured the colored sand of their mandala into the river, Maggie saw the personal forms of her life flowing into the greater river of existence. By releasing attachment to the roles she played, she felt freer to enact the roles of daughter, sister, lover, mother and actress without the limitations of believing she was those roles. After all, she had not adopted the roles in her life for the sake of being a woman, a friend or a coworker. She had taken them on to feel the joy of life flowing through the forms of these roles, to "feel the rapture of being alive," as Joseph Campbell has said.

The more clearly Maggie saw through the roles she played on stage and in daily life, the more clearly she experienced that consciousness was not flowing through a separate, isolated "Maggie." Instead, the life force animating the patterns of her individual roles also animated the roles of every other being in the world. A separate "Maggie" was not releasing her unique self to the cosmos. The pattern of her individuality was the pattern of life itself. She was one of countless patterns through which life experienced the joy and wonder of flowing through itself. In each step of her individual journey, the river of life savored its vitality, creativity, harmony and abundance.

• *Feel the freedom and energy of Release.*
Pattern of Wisdom 23, Release illustrates letting go of treasured experiences to reveal fresh inspirations. Experience this in relation to an uplifting moment such as watching a sunset. Notice if you tried to keep the feeling from slipping away. When the feeling fades, did you attempt to recreate it by reenacting the situation? Feel how your inspiration was not in the colors of the sunset, but in the consciousness seeing the colors. Recall other inspiring moments. See that your experiences are not in the moments, but in the consciousness sensing them. Experience how releasing these moments does not dissolve your consciousness. It frees you to feel the life force flowing through you.

24

EVER DEEPENING

Pattern of Wisdom 24, Ever Deepening illustrates the unending awakenings of consciousness that occur when we experience it shimmering in every person, place and event. At this stage of the human journey, faces and clothing, houses and forests, become vividly alive. Colors glow more vibrantly. Sounds resonate more richly. Flavors satisfy more thoroughly. Appreciation of life shines more fully. Love for others radiates with more connection. As we journey through *24 Patterns of Wisdom*, we see how visible forms point the way to invisible consciousness. Common objects serve as windows for framing openings to energy and intelligence. Exploring the intimate relationship between consciousness and material forms, we sense distinctions dissolving between consciousness and common objects. In a chair, for example, we see the intimate relationship between the energy and intelligence shaping the chair and the shape of the chair's seat, legs and back. As a result, the physical world becomes a vibrant embodiment of the currents of consciousness. Conversely, the elusive currents of consciousness become tangible patterns and forms. Physical objects, from spoons to skyscrapers, become instruments of energy and wisdom. Thoughts and gestures become as tangible as stone. Everything becomes an expression of Wordless Wisdom opening to deeper and more expansive levels of itself.

The more Maggie experienced the roles she played on stage and

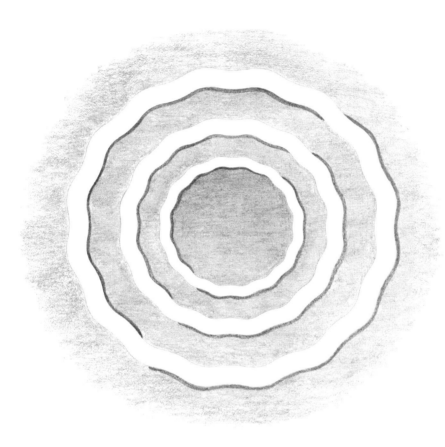

Pattern of Wisdom 24 • Ever Deepening

Passing through wisdom after wisdom reveals unending awakenings.

in daily life as expressions of consciousness flowing within itself, the less she tried to protect herself from the natural currents of change. Instead, she embraced the ongoing process of birth, growth, decay and renewal as the normal yet wondrous interplay of consciousness and matter. She let go of looking for security and wealth in predictable circumstances. Rather, safety and abundance were found in the unbreakable, expansive flow of life within itself. She felt like water cascading down a mountain. The stream of her daily activities encountered bumps and turns, but its current was never broken. In this way, her human journey became a river of consciousness shaping and reshaping itself as it moved through ever-shifting circumstances. The relationships and events that had once seemed solid and unmoving became fluid and ever-changing. The roles and disguises she had assumed in order to access the vitality of consciousness turned out to be themselves made of consciousness.

Passing through wisdom after wisdom, Maggie sensed her life was not moving toward a final wisdom. Realization after realization of consciousness did not arrive at an ultimate experience. Instead, she perceived the unity of matter and consciousness revealing the unfolding of life without end. Her days developed within the continuous Now. Her actions occurred within the limitless Here. Living the paradoxes of individual and cosmos, mundane and miraculous, became as natural as breathing. Instead of seeking material objects, she explored continuous flowerings of possibility. Seeking food and shelter, wealth and creativity, companionship and community changed from fearful struggles into loving engagements with life. The battle to find out who she was, why she was here, and where she was going became an Ever Deepening dance of wonder and gratitude.

• *Sense the ongoing expansion of your life.*
Pattern of Wisdom 24, Ever Deepening illustrates the unending awakening of consciousness. Experience this by recalling the diverse roles you have played on your life journey—child, friend, lover, parent, coworker and more. View these roles as patterns that reveal the flow of life through you. Sense the unbroken stream of this life force flowing from the past, through the present and into the future. Sense it flowing through challenges and awakenings. See these currents of life shimmering through every person you meet and place you go. Imagine this river of consciousness forming and reforming into pattern after pattern of experience without end. Feel this glistening consciousness flowing through all forms and patterns to what is beyond forms and patterns. Sense the peace, vitality and wisdom of being one with consciousness flowing onward though Ever Deepening realms of life.

CONCLUSION

There is an ancient story that is still vital. It describes a young prince who wanders the country doing good. One night, he travels through a forest and comes to a clearing where a salmon is roasting over a fire. The prince is ravenous and grabs a piece of the fish from the spit. The hot salmon burns his fingers and he drops it in his lap, scalding his thigh. The wound is so deep the prince loses his ability to walk. After that, he lives in agony, lying isolated on his bed in the castle. The only thing that soothes the prince's wound is fishing at a nearby lake.

In time, the prince ascends to the throne. As a wounded king, he cannot attend to his realm and the kingdom withers. His castle is the storehouse of the Grail and every night a sumptuous feast is held honoring this treasure. During the feast, the desire of each guest is instantly produced from the Grail. The king is unable partake of the feast and remains in his chamber tending his wound. A local legend describes the one way to heal the king's injury and renew the land. A visitor must attend the Grail Feast and ask the single question that will fathom the depths of the king's distress.

One evening, the king goes fishing on his lake. A young man named Percival wanders by and asks the king if there is a place nearby to spend the night. The king directs him down the road, to the left and across the drawbridge. There, he will see a castle where he can stay. In the castle, Percival attends the Grail Feast. The Grail's beauty is so stunning it leaves him speechless. The next day, he leaves and travels the realm for many years. When he is worn and world weary, Percival returns to the lake where he met the Fisher King. There, a hermit angrily recounts Percival's failure to ask the healing question at the Grail Feast. Percival realizes that this is what he was made for. He hurries to the castle and arrives just in time for the feast. As the Grail is carried into the Great Hall, Percival asks the key question, "Whom does the Grail serve?" Instantly, he realizes the answer: the Grail serves the Grail King. The Fisher King is healed and the land is revitalized.

In this story, the king (or queen) embodies consciousness. The encounter with the salmon depicts the Primal Wound described in Chapter 5. Its fish-like shape is born from an innocent perception of consciousness appearing to split into two circles of Self and Other. The image of the Grail relates to the 24 Patterns of Wisdom presented in this book. Each one is a vessel for accessing the nourishment of consciousness. As long as we see the world through the split lens of the Primal Wound, we cannot receive sustenance from the Grail. The act of fishing to soothe the Primal Wound reflects the ways we try to avoid pain by numbing ourselves with distractions. Percival enacts the tasks of our human journey. Wisdom directs him, and us, to stay on our path, turn toward the invisible forces of consciousness and cross the bridge linking it to the world of visible forms. Like Percival, we can fail to ask the key question that heals our Primal Wound. As a result, we wander the world, passing through countless trials.

At some point, we ask a question that addresses our life quest such as Who am I? Why am I here? Where am I going? In time, we learn this knowledge is not found in physical forms. The wisdom we seek is revealed by experiencing and appreciating the invisible consciousness flowing through physical form.

Like the Grail in the story, *24 Patterns of Wisdom* has described archetypes that help us access the vitality and sustenance of consciousness. To fully experience the knowledge of these archetypes takes both an instant and a lifetime. It is not a linear journey marked in days and years. It is a multi-dimensional space wherein the patterns of wisdom present themselves in unexpected sequences at unforeseen times. They hover just below the surface of every person we meet and place we enter, offering access to deeper harmony, creativity and joy.

This book has endeavored to show you how the 24 Patterns of Wisdom enliven and enrich your life moment by moment. Use these visual symbols daily to experience the patterns of radiant consciousness shaping your home and community, family and friends, work and play. If you encounter challenges on your way, employ these 24 patterns as you would employ wise quotations to comfort and guide you through fear, doubt and confusion. At times of awakening, use the patterns as you would use inspiring icons to honor the beauty and wonder of the human journey. Use them to see the world anew, and enter the renewed life opening before you. With these 24 patterns as your allies, take step after step into the shimmering mystery of consciousness and live the radiant peace and delights of wisdom.

About the Author

Anthony Lawlor's work has been fea-
tured on *The Oprah Winfrey Show* and
National Public Radio. His books include *The Temple in the House* and *A Home
for the Soul*. Lawlor is also an architect
who designs homes, workplaces and
public spaces as environments for recon-
necting with nature, healing our bodies
and enlivening consciousness. During

30 years of architectural practice, he has received awards for excel-
lence in design from such organizations as the American Institute of
Architects and *Interior Design Magazine*. He lectures and offers work-
shops internationally.

In *24 PATTERNS OF WISDOM: Navigating the challenges and
awakenings of the human journey,* Lawlor presents ground-breaking insights into the archetypal design of consciousness. With an architect's
understanding of how patterns of energy and intelligence shape both
human experience and the physical environment, he offers an innovative sequence of visual symbols to guide your passage through common obstacles to expansive realizations. These original symbols serve
as allies for experiencing the radiance, renewing power and wonder
of consciousness in every detail of your life.

For more information visit: patternsofwisdom.com

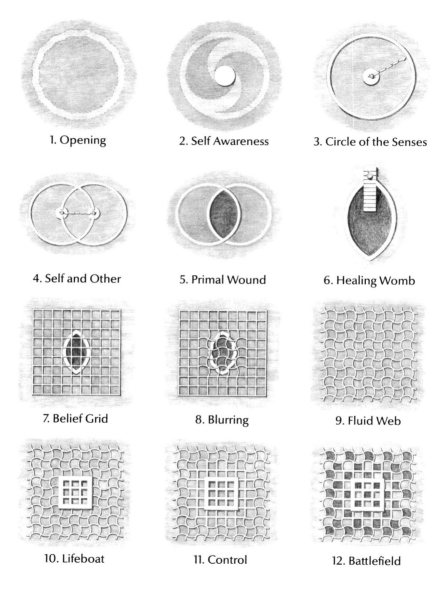

1. Opening

2. Self Awareness

3. Circle of the Senses

4. Self and Other

5. Primal Wound

6. Healing Womb

7. Belief Grid

8. Blurring

9. Fluid Web

10. Lifeboat

11. Control

12. Battlefield

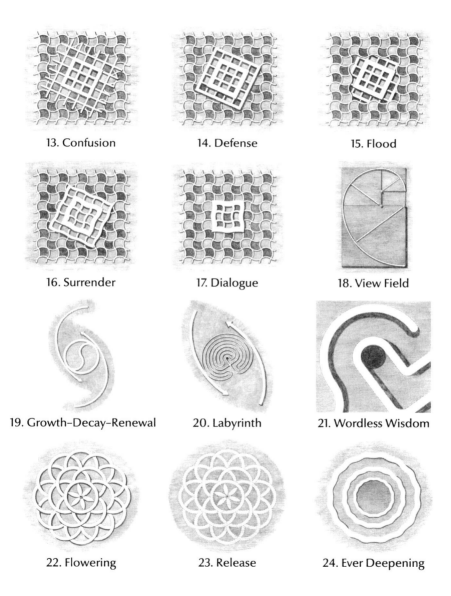

13. Confusion

14. Defense

15. Flood

16. Surrender

17. Dialogue

18. View Field

19. Growth–Decay–Renewal

20. Labyrinth

21. Wordless Wisdom

22. Flowering

23. Release

24. Ever Deepening